THE SWEDES

HOW THEY LIVE AND WORK

Volumes in the series:

The Swedes

HOW THEY LIVE AND WORK

Paul Britten Austin

PRAEGER PUBLISHERS
New York . Washington

BOOKS THAT MATTER

Published in the United States of America in 1970
by Praeger Publishers, Inc.
111 Fourth Avenue, New York, N.Y. 10003

Library of Congress Catalog Card Number: 77-108558

Printed in Great Britain

Contents

List of Illustrations

(Photographs by courtesy of : The Swedish National
Travel Association and The Royal Swedish Embassy)

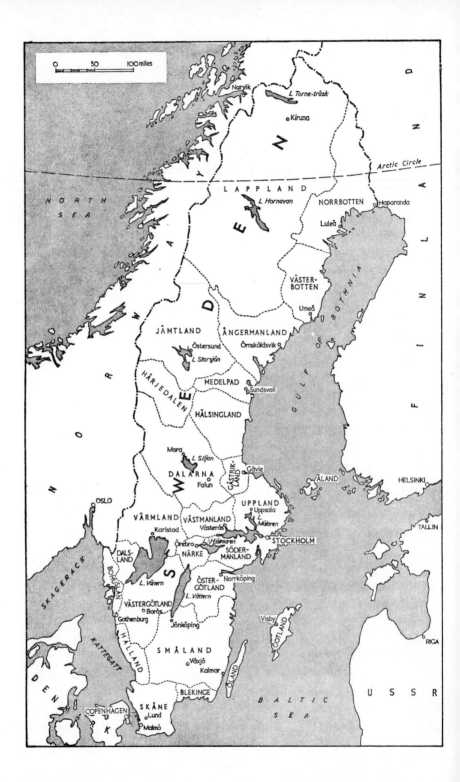

Foreword

THE title of this series seems peculiarly apt to the Swedes, one of the most hard-working peoples on earth. The late President Eisenhower's reference to "a certain Scandinavian country" as an example of socialist disincentive was wide of the mark indeed. Besides, it all depends on what you mean by socialist.

Any book on Sweden's social and economic structure tends to read like a paean of statistical superlatives. This would be wearisome. But Sweden deserves her reputation. In so many ways she is ahead of the rest of us. This is not to say that the very efficiency of the system may not have brought with it grave troubles.

Seventy years ago, far from being the richest country in Europe, Sweden was one of the poorest. No country has ever gone through such swift transformation. From being poor, rural and agrarian, she has become rich, industrialised and urbanised. From being "behind," she has rocketed into the future—and, since we are all interested in the future, it is wise to have a look at Sweden, which in so many ways seems to symbolise it. In this Scandinavian country the inherent logic of modern developments has been speeded up to a quite incredible degree.

Rational social structure and soaring production figures are not, of course, everything. In another place* I have attempted

* Paul Britten Austin: *On Being Swedish; Reflections toward a better understanding of the Swedish character* (Secker & Warburg, and University of Miami Press, Florida)

to trace out what may be the specifically human factors in the Swedish present. This book, like others in the series, is perhaps less about Swedes than about Sweden. Yet few Swedes, I suppose, would be disposed to distinguish between themselves and the society they have built. Their society, in which they take such an intense interest, is their "other self."

P.B.A.

I

The Country and the People

SWEDEN is by far the largest of the five Scandinavian countries. It covers the southern and eastern parts of the Scandinavian peninsula, together with the two large Baltic islands of Gotland and Öland. A glance at the map shows how long and thin the country is. Its area, 173,654 sq miles, makes Sweden the fourth largest country in Europe, only Russia, France and Spain being larger. From its southernmost point, at Ystad, to the remote un-inhabited region of Lapland, where a heap of stones (*Treriks-röset*) marks the point of junction between Sweden, Norway and Finland, the country measures 977 miles. This means that if Sweden could be swung round on its southernmost tip (55° 20' N.), its northernmost point (69° 4' N.) would reach to Naples.

Generally speaking, Sweden may be characterised as a land of immense forests, broken by some 96,000 lakes. Some of these, like the Vänern (Europe's second largest inland water) and the Vättern, are as big as seas. There are also great plains, particu-larly in the south. And great rivers. Only 10 per cent of the land surface is arable and 9 per cent is covered by lakes.

From the plains of Skåne in the far south to the fells and swamps of Lapland in the extreme north there is naturally a very great variation both of scenery and climate. Yet the country's general character is perhaps more definite and un-changing than that of most European countries.

Sweden is not predominantly mountainous. The really Alpine mountain range to the west lies mostly in Norway. These moun-tains are remnants of the Caledonian fold, which in the course of aeons was almost totally stripped of soil, gaining its present form in the Tertiary period. Sweden's own "face" was sculpted by glaciers a million years ago. Scraping away all the loose soil, they deposited instead a thin moraine of weathered and fractured stones of varying size. Glacial rivers left boulder ridges and created deltas, also leaving huge deposits and digging great holes which form today's beautiful lakes. Ever since the last Ice Age, the whole vast slab of primitive rock that is Sweden has slowly been rising, like a piece of rubber depressed by one's thumb, at the rate of about three feet per century. This means that, numerous though the lakes are today, they are much fewer and smaller than they were, for instance, in Viking times. Many of the lakes and creeks (*vik*), over which the Vikings sailed their longships a thousand years ago, are today arable land. For this reason, remains of Viking settlements are usually found on higher ground. They originally lay beside the water's edge.

A glance at the map shows that the great rivers, from which Sweden derives her plentiful supplies of hydro-electric power, all tend to flow in a south-easterly direction, from the Norwegian watershed into the Baltic (called in Swedish *Östersjön*, the East Sea), and the Gulf of Bothnia. The largest are in the north. The highest mountain, Kebnekaise, in Lapland, is only some 7,000 ft high. The rest of Sweden is pleasantly undulating, and in the north hilly.

Scandinavia, generally, has an exceptional climate for its latitude. Lying on the same parallels as Hudson Bay or Alaska, the peninsula is only habitable thanks to the Gulf Stream, which brings warmer air from the west, so that the climate corresponds rather to that of New England than to that of the far north of Canada. A phenomenon entirely due to the latitude is the "Midnight Sun", which can be seen north of the Arctic Circle from mid-May to mid-July. North of that line (66° 30' N.) there is an endless day, when the sun shines for a period of six weeks; and endless semi-night for the corresponding six weeks of mid-winter.

This general contrast between light and darkness, and between warm, even hot, summers and icy winters, is basic to everything in Sweden and seems to affect all aspects of Swedish life. In Stockholm in December the sun, having risen as late as 9.30 a.m., retires below the horizon at 3.30 p.m.—and Stockholm lies a good 700 miles south of the Arctic and the northernmost regions! What winter is like in the far north may therefore be imagined. In the south, it is usually too mild for skiing, but snow is plentiful everywhere else from December (in the far north from September or even August) to April (in Lapland to June). In central Sweden snow still lingers well into April on the northern slopes of hills, where the spring sunshine, falling from a low altitude, cannot get at it to melt it. The 1st of May is regarded not as the first day of summer, as in Britain, but of spring. But the short Swedish summer is lighter, often hotter, and certainly much dryer, than the British. If anyone had so little sense of mood and poetry as to wish to do so banal a thing in so magical an atmosphere, it is possible at midsummer to read a newspaper out of doors in Stockholm at midnight. Even if the Midnight Sun is a phenomenon peculiar to Lapland and the Arctic, there is little difference in climate at that time of year between one part of the country and another; the hottest and driest summer weather is often to be enjoyed in the far north.

Sweden has a very long coastline, indented by archipelagos. Largely uninhabited, these are fearsome threats to shipping in the winter, but a boundless playground for tourists and holidaymakers in the summer. From the air the rocky islands, crowned by stunted conifers, look like an infinite jigsaw puzzle. Starting south of the Norwegian border at Svinesund, the Bohuslän archipelago, with its 2,000 islands, low fiords, skerries and inlets, stretches to just south of Gothenburg, where it gives place to the shallow sandy beaches and dunes of Halland and Skåne provinces. After Malmö, in the extreme south, the archipelago resumes in Blekinge province, in the far south-east, to continue all the way up the east coast to the northernmost point of the Gulf of Bothnia. Stockholm lies about forty miles inland from the outermost skerries, and is therefore not "on the sea," even though its numerous waterways might make it seem so.

Geologically and in every other way the islands of Gotland

and Öland are unlike the mainland. While granite and gneiss are characteristic of all the rest of the country, and everywhere stick out through the soil, Gotland and Öland have a limestone subsoil and are perfectly flat. Gotland's pleasant leafy meadows were compared by the eighteenth-century Swedish botanist Carl von Linné ("Linnaeus") with the Englishman's park, a comparison which to an Englishman perhaps seems far-fetched. Öland is characterised by its steppe-like "alvar," heaths of heather and wild orchids. The long summer days, averaging about 11.5 hours of sunshine in June and not much less in July and August, warm up the tideless sea (nowhere around Sweden's coasts is there any perceptible tide) and give these Baltic islands a much milder climate than the mainland, so that ripe mulberries have been picked in Gotland in October; sheep can graze out of doors all winter, which is not possible anywhere else in central or northern Sweden. Gotland's annual mean temperature (45°F) is the same as in the extreme south of Skåne, as compared with 27°F in the far north.

Administrative divisions

Administratively, Sweden is divided up into twenty-five counties (*län*), of which Stockholm is one. For all practical purposes these *län* have replaced the traditional division—dating back to prehistoric times—into twenty-five provinces (*landskap*), some of which, like Västergötland (the land of the western Goths), were once kingdoms in their own right. The King of Sweden is the titular king of "The Swedes, the Goths and the Vandals," his insignia being the three crowns of those half-legendary kingdoms.

There is also another threefold division; into Norrland, Svealand and Götaland, a division used in weather reports. *Norrland* comprises the six provinces lying along the coast of the Gulf of Bothnia: Gästrikland, Hälsingland, Medelpad, Ångermanland, Västerbotten and Norrbotten, together with the two inland mountainous provinces of Härjedalen and Jämtland; *Svealand* consists of Värmland, Dalarna, Västmanland, Närke, Södermanland, and Uppland provinces; and *Götaland*, the southern part of the country, consists of Skåne, Blekinge, Halland, Bohuslän (all once part of Denmark), Östergötland, Småland, Västergötland, Dalsland, and the islands of Öland and Gotland. Since it is the provincial names which still have emotive and human connotations to the Swedes, I shall use them by preference in this book when referring to different parts of the country.

Stockholm "lies like a ship at anchor" on the waters of Lake Mälaren. It has been the Swedes' capital for over 700 years, and is by general admission one of Europe's most spectacular cities. Built originally on two small islands in the narrows where the waters of the great inland lake system pour out into the archipelago, Stockholm, with its population of 1,268,000 has spread out in recent times to comprise some twenty islands. This makes it a city of wide and, on sunny days, brilliant prospects. In winter the waterways freeze up; but the aspect on a snowy winter's day, in sunshine, is hardly less attractive.

Here the king has his palace and the government its seat. Indeed, this city of a million inhabitants absorbs to itself almost too much of the social and cultural life of a country which in all other respects is exceptionally widely spread out. The more densely populated south, it is true, has its its own "capital" at Malmö and its own university at Lund; and the Gothenburgers, who face westward and can boast of Scandinavia's largest port, (Gothenburg lies almost equidistant from Oslo, Stockholm and Copenhagen), tend to regard their city of just over half a million inhabitants as the capital, if not of Sweden, at least of Scandinavia. Between them and the Stockholmers there is a flourishing rivalry. It is therefore an error to regard Stockholm as the only important Swedish city. Nevertheless, by American or European standards, all Swedish cities are relatively small. Only a dozen have a population of more than 50,000 inhabitants. This does not mean that the social, educational and cultural facilities of many of them would not put many a larger British or American city to shame.

Like the other Scandinavian peoples, the Swedes are one of
the least mixed races in Europe. Their striking appearance,
somewhat less varied than that of many peoples, witnesses to
their common descent. And in fact it is to in-breeding during
the last 5,000 years that the Swedish blonde owes her beauty.
Her earliest known ancestors, fishermen and farmers, arrived
in Sweden after the retreat of the last Ice Age. It is the same
race which inhabits Sweden today.

It is also from that time that the earliest prehistoric remains
date. About 3,000 BC the hunters who had gradually penetrated
northwards in the wake of the receding ice, gained knowledge
of agriculture, and up to a mere sixty years ago most of their
descendants were cultivating the same soil which they originally
broke. Between 1500 and 500 BC the use of bronze gradually
made its appearance, and thereafter that of iron, in which metal
Sweden was to prove so singularly rich.

Lying so far to the north and having such a severe winter
climate, and her soil being relatively poor—the forests were
economically almost wholly worthless—Sweden, up to quite
recently, had experienced almost no immigration, and, over the
centuries, very little invasion. Rather, the land has been a source
of emigration. Exceptions to this outward rather than inward-
flowing pattern have been few. Towards the end of the Middle
Ages, German traders seeking iron, hides and furs—from earliest
times Sweden's main exports—began to penetrate the Baltic
coast, and settled in cities of their own creation. They were
largely responsible for the growth of Stockholm. Medieval Visby,
the Hanseatic port on Gotland, was also an entirely German city.
But the German traders quickly became absorbed into the native
stock, and can hardly be regarded as having constituted a foreign
racial element. In the seventeenth century, too, when Sweden
was a great power, with an empire stretching right across the
north of Europe, there was a certain amount of immigration,

mostly from Germany, the Netherlands, Austria and Scotland.
It is to be noted that these immigrants were called in to provide
much-needed expertise in the running of the administration
and commerce of a country unskilled in such things. Gothenburg,
particularly, owed its development to Dutchmen and Scotsmen,
and even today large numbers of Gothenburgers have such purely
Scottish names as Dickson, McFee and Hamilton. The seventeenth century also saw a sizeable immigration of Walloons,
fleeing from religious persecution in the Low Countries. The
Walloons mostly settled as miners in the Bergslagen district
of central Sweden (southern Dalarna and Västmanland). Again,
there are many Swedish families with Walloon names (Kalvagen,
de Frumerie). Unlike the typical tall slim blond, these Swedes
are of short stature, have brown hair and eyes, and often a
more lively temperament. Some of the most gifted Swedish
families are of Walloon stock.

Not until our own time, when Sweden has suddenly become
one of Europe's most prosperous countries, has there been any
large-scale immigration. Today there are about 300,000 Swedes
of foreign extraction. Many are refugees from Nazi and Communist rule, but their number is swelled by about 10,000 immigrants a year, such as Italians and Yugoslavs, who are being
attracted by high wages and a good standard of living.

In the eighteenth century liberal laws permitted the Jews freedom of religion, and there are a number of Jewish families.
One such is the Bonnier family, who own a very large slice
indeed of the publishing and newspaper industry. But the
Swedish Jews are wholly assimilated, and Sweden can be said
never to have had, or even felt she had, a Jewish problem. A
Swede is usually at a loss to understand why anyone should
discriminate between a Jew and any other European.

The only Swedish racial minority with a distinct profile of
their own are the Lapps. There are about 10,000 *samer*, as they
call themselves, in Swedish Lapland. Their racial derivation,
which appears to be Mongoloid, is a matter of dispute among
the learned, and their language has affinities with Finnish and
nothing in common with Swedish. About 2,000 still lead a

B

nomadic life, following the reindeer up to the mountains in the summertime and back to the lowland forests in winter. Great care has been taken by the Swedish authorities not to assimilate them. On the contrary, everything has been done, at least in recent times, to help them preserve their own culture, language and ways. But the impact of modern civilisation makes their future, as a distinct people and culture, a dubious one. There are also some 35,000 Finns in Swedish Lapland and other parts of the country, and their tongue, which, belonging to the Finno-Ungrarian group, is also utterly distinct from the other Scandinavian languages, has an extraordinary ability to survive in exile.

Finally, it should not be forgotten that about ten per cent of the population of Finland, particularly of the Åland Islands between Sweden and Finland, are of pure Swedish descent, have Swedish names and speak Swedish. Their future as a distinct minority seems uncertain.

★

But if there has been little immigration over the centuries to mix the blood of the Swedes, and hardly any invasions, there have been repeated waves of emigration from a land which at times has been quite unable to support its own birth-rate. The most notable in ancient times was that of the Vikings (AD 800-1000). While the Danish and Norwegian Vikings, and those who came from Bohuslän (*Viken*) on what is now the Swedish west coast, sailed westwards and southwards, plundering the coasts of Europe, founding the Duchy of Normandy and the kingdom of Sicily and occupying half of England, the Swedish Vikings sailed eastwards, founding the state of Russia, which is said to get its name from the *Russ*—red-headed men—of Roslagen county, just north of Stockholm. Navigating Russia by its great rivers, they penetrated as far as Bulgaria and Constantinople.

But the biggest emigration of all was to the United States of America at the end of the nineteenth century. Only Ireland and Norway lost more of their populations to the New World.

Poverty, a rising birth-rate and a falling death-rate, the first impact of industrialism, starvation following a series of bad harvests and, to some extent, oppressive government, were all factors lying behind this mass exodus. The emigration reached its climax in the 1880s, when some 35,000 Swedes were crossing the Atlantic every year. Most settled in the Middle West. In Illinois and Minnesota, still the "Swedish" areas of the United States, the Swedish language, sometimes in archaic and dialect forms, is still spoken by the older generation of Swedish Americans. In all, Sweden lost between a fifth and a quarter of her population.

Today the population is steadily on the rise, not because of the high birth-rate of olden times—in 1960 it reached an all-time low, 13.66 per thousand, then the world's lowest—but thanks to immigration from abroad. The Swede's life-expectancy is also the highest in the world (seventy-five years for men, seventy-nine for women), while the infant mortality rate is the lowest (14.2 per thousand). Such ancient national scourges as tuberculosis have been entirely wiped out. Sweden faces the fact that in the next couple of decades there will be too few Swedes of working age in ratio to pensioners. Without the continued immigration of a good many thousands of foreigners a year the situation would be serious.

The industrialisation and urbanisation of Sweden has occurred with much greater rapidity than that of the major European countries, and the shock effect of so sudden a transition has certainly been responsible for much contemporary Swedish malaise. In the 1880s the urban population constituted no more than fifteen per cent of the whole, and at the turn of the century twenty-two per cent. Today, seventy-five per cent of the Swedish nation lives in towns and cities. For good or for ill, this change has totally shattered the old patterns of Swedish life, and doubtless lies behind many of the problems which notoriously beset Swedish living today and to which the Swedes devote such attention.

There are many areas of Sweden which are being literally depopulated (*avfolkningsbygder*). Their remaining farms are largely inhabited by old people; and indeed for the country as a whole the average age of today's owner-farmer is fifty-three. The young people have moved away from the isolation of the countryside to the towns with their higher standard of living. Fields which their forefathers so painstakingly recovered from the encroaching forest are now being deliberately re-sown with timber-yielding pine and spruce. Uneconomic areas are being deliberately strangled of communications and other services—sometimes in the teeth of loud though unavailing protests. Nevertheless, even though only ten per cent of the country's surface is arable, Sweden is self-supporting in foodstuffs. If she remains so, it is thanks to intense mechanisation of her agriculture.

Population Density

Population density is extremely uneven. In a country more than twice as large as England and Wales put together, there are only about eight million people. Nine-tenths of these live in the southern two-thirds of the country. The vast region of Norrland, more than half the area of Sweden, contains only one-tenth of the population. In Skåne (4,230 square miles) there are nearly twice as many Swedes as there are in the two northernmost provinces (58,000 square miles) of Norrbotten and Väster-botten together. The densest population belt lies between Stockholm and Gothenburg; but no one driving across this stretch of 340 miles of plains and forests would guess as much, or think the countryside anything but very sparsely populated. The average population density, nineteen inhabitants per square mile, does not give a clear idea of how thinly people are spread on the Swedish ground.

There are many factors behind the notoriously high cost of living in Sweden. The lopsidedness of the poulation distribution is certainly one of them. It stands to reason that, where such amenities as the telephone (highest density in Europe, 431 per thousand) TV (255 per thousand) and railways must equally serve the sparsely inhabited wastes of Lapland and the relatively dense urban areas of south and central Sweden, the Stockholmer will in fact not only be paying for his own telephone, but even more for the Laplander's, perhaps a hundred miles of telephone wire being required to bring it to the latter's front door.

LANGUAGE

Swedish belongs to the western branch of the Germanic language. Like Danish, Icelandic and Norwegian, it is a descendant of Old Norse, the common tongue spoken by the Vikings all over Scandinavia a thousand years ago. Some regard it as the purest of the modern Scandinavian languages. That, perhaps, is a matter of opinion. Certainly it is not guttural, like Danish, but clear and limpid, quiet-spoken with a lilt or intonation which is much more difficult for a foreigner to capture than its grammar or pronunciation. On the other hand, Swedish suffers from a shortage of words, a shortage the Swedes have always tried to remedy by liberally adopting and adapting words from foreign tongues. Unlike the Icelanders and Finns, they do not try to find native words for new things and concepts.

This process of assimilating foreign tongues goes back at least as far as the Middle Ages. Towards the end of the Middle Ages, Swedish lost its case-endings. At the same time it adopted from German merchants and administrators many German words (for example, *stad*, town, in lieu of Old Norse *by*, which still means town in Norwegian, but in Swedish has been downgraded to mean village). It also adopted many useful prefixes (*vor—för*) and suffixes. Later, in the seventeenth and eighteenth centuries, the influence of France became paramount. Great numbers of French words were imported, a process which reached its climax in the eighteenth century, when the culture-aspiring Stockholmer used almost as many French words as he did Swedish. After the Franco-Prussian war of 1870, German influence supplanted the French; and in turn was supplanted after 1918 and 1945 by English. A Swedish newspaper today is peppered with Anglo-Saxonisms; but deeper scrutiny reveals the French and German layers beneath. Sometimes the Swede modifies foreign words to his own uses, for example *bil* (car) from *automobil* (plural *bilar*).

One curious feature of the Scandinavian languages is that they add the definite article as a suffix. Thus: *hus* (house), *huset* (the house), *husen* (the houses). *Restaurang* (restaurant), *restaurangen* (the restaurant), *restauranger* (restaurants), *restaurangerna* (the restaurants).

An Englishman or an American finds learning Swedish an interesting experience; he is reminded at every turn how much of his own tongue is in fact Scandinavian. Many English words and expressions, nowadays only used in some particular context, have their everyday Swedish cousins. The word-order, too, is reminiscent of Tudor English. Though Swedish is not a particularly difficult language to learn, its pronunciation—or rather its intonation—has a vaguely sing-song lilt which reminds an Englishman, perhaps, of Welsh and is apt to defeat him.

NATIONAL CHARACTERISTICS

The more isolated a people's history and the more homogeneous its culture, the more distinct is likely to be its character. Swedes, being usually of a highly empirical and scientific turn of mind, tend to deny the existence of any such thing as a national character, or that their own is in any way distinct from that of other Europeans. This is not the impression of those who know them best: the Swede has probably one of the most definite spiritual physiognomies of any European.

For centuries he lived on the outermost periphery of European culture. He divided his time between farming, fishing, warfare and perhaps religion. His tribal enemies were ice, snow and darkness. The Vikings, however heroic a people, and however remarkable their artistic culture may have been, cannot have been very nice people to know—such, as least, was the opinion of those who came so rudely into contact with them. But with the disastrous collapse of the Swedish Empire in the early eighteenth century, and the various wars which followed, all

ending in defeats, the warrior streak in the Swedish character
seems to have come abruptly to an end. For a hundred and
fifty years, at least, the Swedes have been neutral; and this
neutrality, reinforced by their geographical apartness, seems
to have permeated their blood. What characterises—or up to
the latest generation has characterised—the modern Swede has
been a peculiar objectivity and detachment. The scientific and
technical spirit sets its stamp on all he does.

Not only does he regard the outside world with something of
the detachment—and perhaps the sense of superiority—natural
in a neutral watching other nations periodically tearing each
other to pieces, but he looks at himself in much the same way.
At the same time, the precipitate industrialisation and urbanisation of his society has uprooted most of his traditional values
and turned a thrifty and somewhat hard-working peasant into
an affluent, ambitious, over-organised, sometimes over-strained
townsman. Like many other recently industrialised peoples, the
Swedes, one can say, have still hardly learned to live in towns.
As if conscious of this, they return to their beautiful, unpolluted
country, to "nature," on the least pretext.

For behind the rather blank, formal, meticulous and retiring
(Swedes say shy) exterior, there is another Swede: chaotically
emotional, prone to melancholy, to lyrical enthusiasms, to poetry,
song and liquor. Between the two Swedes who go about pre-
tending to be one and the same person (with a functional
"title" stuck on to him, by which he must be addressed—
"direktör," "professor," etc), one senses a gap, and a great
uncertainty. Swedes lament their lack of a humanistic tradition,
and are rapidly trying to acquire one. Certainly they are not
good psychologists, and can find the realm of ordinary human
intercourse hard to fathom.

Behind his perfectionism, however, which is one of his prime
traits, there lies very often a fairly naïve and simple-hearted
fellow, a good deal less complex than other Europeans, and with
neither the sometimes vicious sophistication of the Anglo-Saxon,
nor his inbred double-think. This, perhaps, is why Swedes get on
so well in the United States, to whose culture they seem to have

contributed some essential and valuable traits. Open-mindedness, after all, is a great virtue.

Another trait which seems to distinguish the Swede, at least from the Englishman or American, is his capacity for corporate thinking and action. Englishmen and Americans are apt to find Sweden over-organised, and cannot understand the pleasure the Swede finds in organising it still further. But the Swede has an almost medieval sense of corporate feeling, and it has paid handsomely in the solution of many social and economic problems which elsewhere have proved intractable. Perhaps he makes up for a certain lack of personal communion with his fellows on the individual plane by a strong feeling of social identification. This does not mean that a Swede does not value his own personal freedom. He does, in high degree. Indeed, it has been paradoxically said that he is every bit as much an anarchist as a socialist.

A last trait which should be noted is the peculiar fondness, or at least deference, which Swedes have traditionally felt for foreigners. This goes back at least to the Middle Ages, when a Stockholm monk inscribed on the walls of Stockholm Cathedral "a preference for and favouritism of foreigners" among what he considered to be the vices of the Swedish nation. Perhaps it is that, once he can speak the foreigner's language, the Swede feels, in a way, more at ease with him than with other Swedes, towards whom he often stands in a formal relation that is almost Japanese. With the big influx of foreigners since the war, however, this attitude is changing.

So is much else. The motor car and TV have opened up the country, and the Swedes, from being isolated, have become the most travelled people in Europe. They are gaining an ease of manner and a self-assurance largely lacking in the older generation, of whose stiffness and stand-offishness the youngest generation are consequently highly critical. The revolution in education, from the old Prussian examination system to a more liberal American style of schooling, is likely to accentuate the change.

In a word, Sweden is hurriedly coming into Europe and

the world at large; and this experience, together with the other traumatic changes in Swedish society and culture, is likely to produce quite another sort of Swede from either the ancient Viking or the formalistic, meticulous, slightly melancholy personage the world has hitherto known as "the Swede."

One last point. A great deal has been written in the British and American popular press about the Swedish suicide rate. This is one of those labels which, whether justified or not, tend to stick to a country. In point of fact it is almost impossible to make realistic statistical comparisons between different countries, because of different methods of keeping account of such matters, different religious attitudes, falsifying of figures, etc. The "jolly" Danes in fact have a higher rate, and so do half a dozen other nations; several American states have suicide rates comparable to Sweden's. On the other hand, the Swedish rate (nineteen per thousand) is high; according to an American psychologist who has studied the matter, it is attributable chiefly to ego-failure when ambitions are frustrated.* This would seem in keeping with the general tendency to be perfectionist. The murder rate (sixty-two per 76,661 deaths in 1964) is only one-tenth of the American.

HISTORICAL LANDMARKS

Though their earliest records are limited to the Icelandic sagas and the 2,000 runestones scattered about the countryside, the history of the Swedes may be said to begin with the Vikings. True, seven hundred years before, Tacitus (AD 98) had written of the "Sueones," a people inhabiting the region just north of present-day Stockholm. He describes them as a people "mighty in men and in ships." By Viking times this people had grown into a well-stratified society. As the wealth from the Viking raids poured in, an originally egalitarian peasant society changed. Already the wealthy peasants (*storbönder*), whose descendants

* Herbert Hendin: *Suicide and Scandinavia*. New York and London, 1964.

were to become the Swedish aristocracy of medieval times, had several well-defined classes beneath them, the lowest being slaves. The *Svear*—as these people were called—elected their kings, who, however, were mostly commanders-in-chief in time of war. They worshipped the old Norse gods. Tor, Odin, Freya, etc., and in a sacred grove at Old Uppsala hung the bodies of their human sacrificial victims.

In the ninth century the Christian missionaries arrived. The first was Ansgar who, about AD 830, founded the earliest Christian church in the trading centre of Birka, on an island in the Mälaren lakes. Not until 1164, however, did Sweden receive its first archbishopric, at Uppsala. By then, after a long struggle, the old religion had been ousted, at least nominally. The conflict is reflected in the runestones, many of which still bear Tor's hammer, while others are inscribed with the cross of the "White Christ."

In the eleventh century King Erik the Holy carried a crusade into Finland, which he conquered and which, until the Russians wrested it from Sweden at the beginning of the nineteenth century, was to remain a Swedish province.

The Vikings' prosperity had been due to the closing of the Mediterranean trade routes to western shipping by the Arabs. About 1096 the first crusade reopened them, and thereafter the Russian route, which the Swedes had dominated, ceased to have much importance.

Christianity led to a reinforcement of the royal authority. From being based on possession of land, wealth changed into possession of capital. German traders penetrated the Swedish coasts, and small cities grew up. Stockholm is said to have been founded in or about 1255 by Birger Jarl, replacing the earlier capital at Sigtuna, on Lake Mälaren.

In 1389, for the first and only time, the Kalmar Union united Scandinavia under a single crown: the Danish. There followed a century-long struggle. While the Swedish aristocracy ambiguously tried to serve both Swedish interests and their own, the miners of Bergslagen and Dalarna, whose interests lay with the Hanseatic city of Lübeck, which imported their iron, became increasingly hostile to the Danish pretensions. Under their leader Engelbrekt they rose against the Union (1434-36) and nearly succeeded in smashing it.

It was not until the 1520s, however, that Gustavus Vasa, (1523-60), at last succeeded in ousting the Danes and establishing his own absolute authority. Sweden finally became an independent centralised state. The last straw had been the "Bloodbath of Stockholm" (8 November, 1520) when the Danish king Christian the Tyrant beheaded eighty-two of the Swedish leaders. Aided financially by Lübeck, Gustavus Vasa recaptured the capital and threw the Danes out of the country. The Kalmar Union was finally at an end.

But debts had placed Gustavus in the thrall of Lübeck, and to liquidate them he seized the property of the Church. Sweden, however, did not immediately, or even willingly, become Protestant, and the establishment of the religious hegemony of the Swedish State Church was a fairly long and complex process. Gustavus also had to crush a rising of the peasants (1543) who had originally supported him. The outcome of the struggle was that the crown and the aristocracy consolidated their power, while the losers in the struggle for national liberty were the peasants.

Further civil war followed in the reign of Gustavus's unbalanced son Erik XIV (1560-68), who was finally deposed and probably poisoned by his brother, the Catholic Johan III (1568-92). Charles IX (1599-1611), a Calvinist, attempted to heal the religious schism, without effect. Finally the Swedish Church, which from the days of Gustavus Vasa had been strongly influenced by German Lutheranism, was made a vassal of the State, with a rigidly Lutheran dogma. To it all Swedes thenceforth were bound by law to adhere.

In the seventeenth century, Sweden's participation on the Protestant side in the Thirty Years' War, under the leadership of her great king Gustavus II Adolphus, "The Lion of the North" (1611-32), made her a great power, with possessions all round the Baltic and in Germany. The aristocracy, particularly, enriched themselves. From this time date most of the great manor houses of central Sweden, and many Swedish churches still contain magnificent works of art looted from such places as faraway Czechoslovakia.

Gustavus Adolphus, killed in a cavalry charge at the Battle of Lützen (1632), was succeeded by his six-year-old daughter Christina. During her minority (1632-44) the realm was ruled by the great chancellor Axel Oxenstierna. By now the aristocracy had come to own seventy-two per cent of the Swedish soil, while the burden of taxation fell exclusively on the peasantry. The abdication of the eccentric, bohemian and intellectual queen, and her conversion to Catholicism (1654), was one of the most sensational events of Swedish history. By the Peace of Roskilde in 1658 Skåne and the southernmost provinces of present-day Sweden were wrested from the Danes. In 1680, Charles XI (1660-97) sharply reduced the possessions of the aristocracy and restored the crown's authority, the Swedish soil thereafter being owned equally by crown, aristocracy and peasantry. The Carolinian dictatorship had been established.

Charles XI's successor, Charles XII (1697-1718) was one of the greatest conquerors Europe has ever known. After great successes against the Danes and the Russians, however, his forces were finally and resoundingly defeated at Poltava (1709) in Russia, and the king himself and a fragment of his army retreated into Turkey. The rest capitulated. In 1715, Charles, with two aides, returned to Sweden. While besieging the fortress of Fredrikshald (Halden) in Norway, the king was shot dead in the trenches. The wars which had cost Sweden 30,000 slain were at last at an end. So was the Swedish Empire.

The eighteenth century was the era of Sweden's first—not very successful—experiments in parliamentary government. They degenerated into ruthless struggles between the Francophile "Caps" and the Russophile "Hats." For sixty years the great powers of Europe, anxious that Sweden should never rise again as a military power, pulled all the strings of Swedish politics. But the Age of Freedom was also the age of the great botanist Carl Linnaeus (1707-1778), of K. V. Scheele (1742-1786) the chemist, and of the first flourishing of Swedish art and science.

As elsewhere in Europe, it also saw the rise of the Third Estate —the bourgeoisie. The Age of Freedom was brought to an end in 1772 with a *coup d'état* by the brilliant and histrionic Gustaf III. Gustaf was to rule, first as an enlightened dictator, then as a less enlightened one, for twenty years. In the end he was shot down by an assassin at a masquerade ball in his own opera house in 1792.

But the Gustavian Age is not remembered so much for Gustaf's political mistakes—he allied himself with an aristocracy that hated him, instead of with the rising middle class—as for its extraordinary cultural flowering. Those were the days of the great painter Elias Martin, the sculptor Tobias Sergel, and Sweden's immortal song-writer Carl Michael Bellman. Gustaf founded the Royal Dramatic Theatre, the Opera and the Swedish Academy and was himself an actor, producer and dramatist of distinction. He was succeeded by the eccentric Gustaf IV Adolf (1792-1809), whose anti-Napoleonic policies led Sweden to the brink of ruin and the final loss of Finland (1809). Deposed, Gustaf Adolf was replaced by the volatile Napoleonic marshal Bernadotte (Karl XIV Johan [1818-44]), who was elected Crown Prince by the Riksdag (Parliament) in 1809, and invited to come and restore the country's fortunes, which by able administration he largely did. At the same time a new constitution was adopted, from which the present one has developed. Bernadotte was also the originator of Swedish neutrality. Less happily, he exchanged Finland for Norway, which was united under one crown with Sweden until 1905.

It has only been in our own time that Sweden's age-old poverty has given place to prosperity. The first stimulus was a tremendous rise in the European demand for timber. The invention of the steam sawmill freed forestry from its dependence on water power, and all along the coast of the Gulf of Bothnia great sawmills grew up. Between 1830 and 1860 timber exports multiplied six times. At the same time the invention of the Bessemer process made it possible for the Swedes to make high-grade steel from their own iron ore, and the Thomas process and the arrival of railways (1850) enabled them to exploit the great seams of high-content ore in Lapland.

During the nineteenth century the middle classes demanded ever more political influence. In 1866 the old Four Estate Riksdag (nobles, clergy, burghers and peasants) was replaced by a two-chamber parliament. Against the expectations of the commercial classes, however, this led not to a rise in their own power, but in that of the peasants. Meanwhile a new class was making its appearance: the industrial proletariat. The first trade union came into being in the 1880s, strongly supported by the free churches, which had enjoyed a right to exist since 1858. Not until 1901, however, did truly democratic representation make its breakthrough. Based on the motto "one gun, one vote" it was a function to some extent of conscription, introduced at that time.

In 1905, after some heart-burnings, the Union with Norway came peacefully to an end. It was the first case in modern history of one nation giving another its liberty without an armed struggle.

The world economic crisis of 1909 led to a great strike, involving 300,000 workers. Although it failed in its immediate objects, the extension of the vote that same year to all men over twenty-four years of age opened the way to a democratic régime which would eventually largely resolve the social problems of the age. In 1919 women were given the vote, and the electorate was thereby expanded to comprise fifty-four per cent of the population.

Sweden's neutrality in World War I was far from being a happy one. Mistaken policies led to widespread economic distress, and gave the Swedes a lesson in the art of neutrality which they applied with effect in World War II. The great political figure immediately after the Great War was the socialist leader Hjalmar Branting (who died in 1925). He broke with the Communists, opted for social democracy by reform rather than by revolution, and led the Social Democratic movement into the paths it has followed ever since.

The economic crises of the early 1920s were followed by a

period of unprecedented prosperity. Swedish neutrality had left Swedish industry unimpaired and able to exploit the great post-war economic expansion. The twenties were the age of Ivar Kreuger, "The Swedish Match King." Kreuger, who became one of the leading figures of international finance, finally bought up almost the entire world's match industry; but he also played fast and loose with his own companies' accounts. A victim of the Great Depression and his own criminal manipulations, Kreuger committed suicide in Paris in 1932.

It was at the height of the depression that the Social Democratic leader Per Albin Hansson formed the first Social Democratic government (1932). By allying his party with the farmers, he gained sufficient power in the Riksdag to initiate welfare policies which, under uninterrupted Social Democratic governments, have been extended ever since.

On the outbreak of World War II, Sweden, like the other Scandinavian countries, again declared herself neutral. But while Denmark and Norway were invaded by the Germans in April 1940, and Finland by the Russians in 1939, Sweden was fortunate in not being attacked. There followed some anxious years, when the country was entirely surrounded by potential enemies, a situation in which the Swedes were obliged to make concessions to the Germans—the so-called transit traffic of German troops by train to and from Norway through West Sweden being naturally a cause of great bitterness in Norway; on the other hand, the Swedes did what they could to help their Scandinavian brethren. Since the war Sweden has declined membership in the Atlantic Pact, and has followed a policy of "west-oriented alliance-free neutrality," putting her trust chiefly in the balance of power between East and West, and in the United Nations, of which she is a most active member.

The Swedes, that is, interpret their neutrality in an active, not a passive sense. It gives them the right, they feel, and even the duty, of having—and expressing—an opinion of their own on the world's affairs. As is only to be expected, this sometimes brings them into bad odour both with the Russians and the Americans. On the other hand, Stockholm tends to become the rallying point of many forces from "The Third World," who here find sympathy for the plight of the oppressed peoples and—oddly enough in so wealthy a western country—radical attitudes not dissimilar to their own.

———

View of central Stockholm from the Kaknäs TV tower. In the distance is Lake Mälaren; in the middle foreground are the Royal Palace, the Riksdag Buildings and the Town Hall with its striking tower.

The Arendal shipyard in Gothenburg turns out supertankers. Assembled section by section, the completed vessel is gradually pushed out down the slipway.

2

How the Country is Run

THE CONSTITUTION

SWEDEN has the oldest written constitution in Europe. Officially, the Social Democrats, who have been in power ever since 1932, are dedicated to the abolition of the monarchy. But Sweden is still a kingdom, and appears likely to remain one. The present prime minister, Mr Tage Erlander, is quoted as having said: "Yes, I'm a republican, of course. But no, I don't think I want a republic." Even in the late 1960s publicity polls among the younger generation revealed that King Gustav VI Adolf, an admired octogenarian of immense vigour, who came to the throne in 1950 after the very long reign of his father Gustav V (1907-50), is one of the most popular people in the country.

Studsvik Nuclear Energy Centre, in typical Swedish landscape.

c

In practice, the 1809 constitution has been much modified, and is currently being rewritten to bring it into line with realities. Its basic principle is a balance of power between a parliamentary legislature, a royal administration, and an independent judicature. Although all law is made, and the country is governed, in his name, the king wields no personal power whatever. Unlike the British monarch, however, he sits with the cabinet at its Friday meetings, and acts as its ex-officio chairman. It is with the cabinet (*kungl. majestät*—"the royal majesty") that all real power resides. All cabinet ministers are appointed by the prime minister (*statsministern*), who is the leader of the political party commanding the most effective majority in the parliament (*Riksdag*)

The Riksdag has two chambers, an upper and a lower. Each is elected, alternately, at four-yearly intervals, by all Swedes over twenty years of age. There are 151 seats in the upper chamber and 233 in the lower. Their authority is equal, and in order to become law a bill must pass both. If the houses cannot agree then a Bill (*motion*) only survives if compromise can be reached in committee. Financial decisions require an aggregate vote of both houses, and legislation is usually debated simultaneously in both chambers. While the lower (*andra kammaren*) is elected directly on a national basis, the upper (*första kammaren*) is elected successively, one-eighth of its members being chosen annually in general but indirect elections, the city and county councillors being the electors. Since this system is felt to be unwieldy, an agreement exists among the political parties to change over to a single-chamber system as from 1971.

There are (in 1969) five political parties, represented in the Riksdag as follows: *Social Democrats*, upper chamber, seventy-nine seats, lower 125; *Central Party* (formerly the Farmers' Party), upper thirty-one, lower, thirty-nine; *Liberals* (Folkpartiet), upper twenty-five, lower thirty-four; *Conservatives* (Högern), upper twenty-five, lower thirty-two; *Communists*, upper one, lower three. In the 1968 elections to the lower chamber there seemed to be a prospect of the long Social Democratic reign at last being brought to a close by a combined onslaught of their "bourgeois" (Liberal, Centre, Conservative) opponents. But the invasion of Czechoslovakia and the Socialists' able political manoeuvring led to a resounding Social Democrat victory. The régime has a comfortable majority in both houses, enabling it to go on with its social welfare policies for another four-year term. Of the total votes, the Social Democrats won 50.1 per cent, which, by the rules of the Swedish parliamentary game, gives them a clear mandate. The "bourgeois" opposition, bitterly defeated just when it was relying on at last getting into power, has tried to sink its differences in time for the next struggle. Clearly, about half the population is pro-socialist.

The legislative process

The Riksdag's chief function is to analyse legislation, notably the budget. Characteristic of the Swedish parliamentary system is the great amount of work done in committee. By the time a Bill has reached the stage of being debated in the Riksdag, it has gone a long way. American filibuster tactics are impossible, and the outcome is usually foreseeable.

Between a Bill's initial stages and its final implementation as law, there is a highly characteristic process, peculiar to Swedish legislation. The first step is the setting up of an *utredning* (a direct translation of the word would be unravelment, disentanglement) —a parliamentary commission. In such commissions, jointly formed of members of both houses, all parties are proportionately represented. Some are standing committees. Others are set up for particular purposes. In either case, they work on the "*remiss*" system. This means that every conceivable organisation and public or private body likely to have a special interest in the proposed reform is asked to submit its views.

It is said that every Swede belongs on an average to at least three organisations—professional, educational, sporting, or some other interest-group. This flora of bodies, known loosely as *Organisationssverige* ("Organisation-Sweden") takes up ten pages of small type in the Anglo-Swedish dictionary. Authors and acousticians, botanists and Baptist churches, sheep-breeders and handicraft industries, amateur dancers and minigolf enthusiasts, all have their own interest-organisations. Some, like the Confederation of Trades Unions (LO), are of maximal, others of minimal, importance. But all, whether asked for their opinion or not, may independently raise their sectional voices on legislation. Finally, the members of the Commission, together with such experts as they may have co-opted, produce their proposals. Often a dissident minority opinion is attached. This provides the motivation of the Bill and, for the judiciary, an indication of the sense in which it is to be interpreted, should it become law. The Bill itself is not prepared by the Commission. That is the function of the Ministry concerned.

From this it will be seen that the Swede, in his parliamentary democracy, is actually represented twice over, once through his political party, and again thanks to the *remiss* system. In highly controversial questions, such as the changeover to right-hand driving, there is yet a third method : the plebiscite. But this is only occasionally used, and its results are not legally binding on the Government. The plebiscite does not play the same role in Swedish affairs as it does in Swiss.

Once passed by the Riksdag and signed by the king-in-cabinet, the law is not implemented by the ministry which has prepared it, but by a public-service agency. Anyone visiting a Swedish government ministry is likely to be amazed at its small size—a cabinet minister usually has no more than about a hundred staff at his beck and call. There are eleven such ministries : Foreign Affairs, Justice, Defence, Social Affairs, Communications, Finance, Education and Ecclesiastical Affairs, Agriculture, Commerce, Home Affairs and Health. What they administer is not the law, but the public-service boards (*styrelser*), subject in each case to their authority. Thus, the great school reform is currently being administered, not by the Ministry of Education, but by the National Board of Education (*Skolöverstyrelsen*). The only ministry which—for obvious reasons—does not function in this way is the Ministry for Foreign Affairs (*Kunglig Utrikesdeparte-mentet*—UD). All others use public-service agencies. Thus, under the Ministry for Social Affairs, Labour & Housing come the Social Welfare Board, the Social Insurance Board, the Workers Protection Board, the Labour Market Board, the Housing Board, and certain other smaller agencies. In 1968-69 this ministry had at its disposal Sw. cr. 10,662 million (£853 million, $2,132 million), or more than a quarter of the entire national budget. Although immediately responsible to the minister, the director general of each of these boards in practice enjoys a great deal of autonomy.

By long tradition the Swedish civil service is apolitical. Even in the ministries the under-secretaries of state—one per ministry —are the only political appointees; and not all of them are noted for their political affiliations. Any Swedish civil servant is free to engage in politics on his own account, or even hold political office, provided that his political interests do not become confused with his job in the civil service.

All the public-service boards are under an obligation to co-operate with one another, without reference upwards to their ministries. Their directors-general, usually but not invariably political appointees, hold office for a six-year period. Any board's decisions may be appealed against to a higher authority—that is, to the ministry. By ancient tradition, any Swedish citizen has the right to *gå till kungen*—appeal direct to the king, which today means to the cabinet. Quite trivial and individual matters are sometimes dealt with at this level. More normally, they are dealt with by administrative courts, whose decisions are final.

Swedish civil servants also enjoy remarkable security of tenure of office. They cannot be dismissed without trial. On the other hand, they are personally accountable. Any civil servant may be sued for abusing his powers. A further check on their activities is provided by the remarkable law which makes all public documents—matters of national security only excepted—open to inspection by any member of the public. In practice, no doubt, the right is exercised only to a limited extent. Still, it exists.

THE OMBUDSMAN

Another very important bulwark against abuse of power—recently imitated in Britain—is the office of *Ombudsman* (literally *Justitieombudsman*, "the representative of justice"). He is coeval with the 1809 constitution. No one knows who first thought him up. But from the outset he has played a most important part in Swedish affairs.

The *ombudsman* is a high-ranking judge. Commanding the confidence of all parties in the Riksdag, he is appointed by it for a four-year period, and has almost autocratic powers. His special and over-riding duty is to see that the letter of the law is applied. In a country where the bureaucrat has his finger in so many pies, his significance has steadily risen; so has the scope of his activities. Every year, either on his own initiative or at the request of injured parties, the JO and his assistants look into some 1,000 cases. He can call for any documents and summon any witness. His decisions take the form of a "reminder"—a reasoned comment on an official's conduct. Addressed to the official in question, this reminder expounds the law to him, and points out in what respect he has failed to abide by it. It is not usual, except in grave cases, for the *ombudsman* to institute judicial proceedings. Although he cannot himself reverse any decision of a court of law, he may however petition the government, the Riksdag or any of the public-service agencies to do so.

Each year the JO presents his report to the Riksdag. It can make most interesting reading. In all his 160 years of existence there is no evidence that political pressure has ever been brought to bear on an ombudsman—a fair indication of the esteem in which the office is held, and the strong tradition of impartiality in Swedish administration. The only persons in Sweden exempt from his "reminders" are the king and the cabinet.

The very existence of the ombudsman, the knowledge that he is on the watch, is a check on the vagaries of bureaucracy.

For instance the Malmö chief of police recently made regulations preventing youths on motor-bikes from roaring down the city streets at night, disturbing the sleep of peaceful citizens. His action was widely applauded, and other district police chiefs began to emulate it. But however admirable, it was not legal. No Swedish law gives chiefs of police the right to block the king's highway to noisy youths, or indeed to anyone else. The ombudsman intervened, and the chief of police was fined. It is not for police chiefs to legislate.

LOCAL GOVERNMENT

If Sweden, unlike Switzerland, has a very old tradition of highly centralised administration, she has an even older tradition of local government. In early times the various provinces each had their own legal codes. Today there is only one law for the whole country; but the twenty-five *län* (counties), though in many respects responsible to the central administration, nevertheless to a great degree manage their own affairs. It has, however, recently become a matter of some anxiety that Swedes do not seem to be taking quite such a fervid interest in local government as they used to do, but tend to leave vital matters to the central authorities.

Each *kommun* (municipality) is regarded as self-governing in local matters; roads, water supply, sewerage, basic education, child welfare, etc, are all administered locally. Of the 1,000 such *kommuner*, some are so small as to have only some 200 inhabitants. The requirements of such crucial innovations as the new school reform, however, have necessitated mergers of the very smallest. Heavily subsidised by the State, the communes levy income tax in the light of local conditions. About half a Swede's income tax goes to the State, and half to his *kommun*; therefore some Swedes are taxed more heavily than others, according to where they live. On the other hand, no rates are levied on property, as is done in Britain.

Each county (*län*) is presided over by a *landshövding* (lord lieutenant, governor). Usually an experienced ex-politician, his reward has been to be appointed by the government to such a post for life. The *landshövding* is also the central government's representative in the county, and sits as chairman of the locally-elected county council (*länsstyrelse*). His personality and political tinge are, of course, matters of some importance in local affairs.

Further integration with central government policy is secured via the regional branches of the public-service agencies. All hospitals, for instance, are the responsibility of the county councils. So are schools. But their operation is kept in line with overall national policy via the local offices of the *Skolöverstyrelsen* and the *Medicinalstyrelsen*, whose officers act as advisers and interpreters of the regulations.

The division of the whole country into communes (*kommuner*) dates from 1863. As the flight from the countryside, and the simultaneous growth in a commune's duties, had led to mergers, their numbers have been steadily decreasing. At present the primary local government bodies of Sweden consist of 133 towns (*städer*), ninety-six market towns (*köpingar*), 777 rural communes and twenty-three urban districts (*municipalsamhällen*). The smaller rural communes are being encouraged, but not forced, by the central government to collaborate in "blocks" based on common interests, through joint committees. The whole three-fold division into towns, rural communes and urban districts is currently being questioned, however, and as society has changed it is possible that it is a distinction which has lost much of its real meaning.

Under the Local Government Act of 1955 all primary communes have the same powers. Their authority in all matters lying outside the scope of the provincial authorities, though absolute, is defined by the Act, and their decisions may only be challenged by someone living within the commune. If unchallenged, even where illegal, such decisions remain in force. A good example of this was the decision of many Swedish communes in 1953, after the great Dutch flood disaster, to send financial aid to their Dutch colleagues. In a few communes this act of generosity was challenged by individuals on the ground that the law only permits communes to spend public money to their electors' direct advantage. Where the gifts were challenged they were annulled by the Supreme Administrative Court (*Regeringsrätten*). Elsewhere they were made.

A commune's duties are in part obligatory, in part optional. Under the former heading fall social welfare, schools, public health, drainage, fire brigades, etc. Under the latter are such matters as the provision of libraries, sports grounds, swimming pools, ice-hockey rinks, community centres and so forth. Generally speaking, the communes have not been backward in providing these social and cultural amenities, and some of the wealthier, notably of course the cities (*städer*), have been lavish. There are towns which positively pride themselves on their achievements in this field, and are justifiably famous for them. Örebro is a town speckled with public works of art, and having a magnificent community centre and theatre; and in Eskilstuna one-third of all the children are engaged in some sort of voluntary musical activity.

The competency of the twenty-five secondary or county communes (*landsting*) was formerly limited to maintaining hospitals; but this has recently been extended to cover mental hospitals, nursing, dental care, midwifery and maternal welfare. But the *landsting* have no authority over the primary, local communes.

All communal bodies are elected on a four-year basis. They are either legislative or administrative. The former (*kommunalfullmäktige*) are elected by proportional representation, and their number of members is in ratio to the number of inhabitants. Thus a commune of 2,000 persons will have a council of some fifteen to thirty councillors, while larger ones will have councils of up to sixty. Stockholm, the largest, is exceptional in that its city council, which sits in the magnificent council chamber of the spectacular Town Hall, has 100 members. Communal electors must be Swedish citizens, registered in the commune, and not less than twenty-three years of age. Bankrupts may not vote. Nor are the highest officials eligible for election. But no one else under the age of sixty, if elected, may decline office, a curious throwback to medieval practice in, for instance, British towns. Sessions are held in public, between five and ten times a year. The chairman, elected by the council, holds office for a year, and is the commune's representative on all public occasions. The council exercises the power of levying local taxes. But though individual assessments of income are made by the State, the *skattekrona*—or percentage of income liable to tax—is decided annually by the council of the commune.

The administrative body is the *kommunalnämnd*, in towns known as the *drätselkammare* (treasury office), in Gothenburg and Stockholm as the *stadskollegium*. This executive council directs the administration of the commune's affairs and supervises the activities of other committees, whose members are chosen from it. Some of these committees are compulsory and required by statute, and are more or less independent of the council; they carry out their business within the terms of current legislation. The only hold the council has over them is in granting or withholding funds. Other committees, mostly those administering cultural and free-time facilities, are voluntary. Both sorts of committee may co-opt persons who are not members of the council.

While most expenditure is covered by local taxation, the communes receive substantial grants from the State, for instance for teachers' salaries, school buildings, public premises, certain forms of public assistance and child welfare, homes for the aged, etc. Communal borrowing, if of a certain size or having a term of repayment of more than five years, is also subject to State approval.

All communes belong to the Association of Swedish Communes. It not only looks after their common interests, but also, in the form of a limited company, conducts central purchasing operations on their behalf. Their employees, too, belong to a national trade union of communal employees (*Kommunaltjänstemannaförbundet*).

THE JUDICIARY

The independence of the third arm of government, the judiciary, is as cardinal a point of Swedish law as it is of British.

To be a judge in Sweden, however, is not a form of promotion for lawyers but a profession in itself. Many judges are quite young men and women. A Swedish law court also studiously avoids all the bewigged pomp and circumstance of a British court, and likewise eschews the rhetoric and emotional overflow of a French one. Nor can a Swede swallow the idea that any magistrate should be a member of the police force. The atmosphere is clinical and remarkably dispassionate.

The lowest level of the judicial hierarchy is the 120 Rural Courts of First Instance. Presided over by one judge, sitting alone, they are competent to try both civil and criminal cases. In more important cases the judge is aided by three to nine lay assessors. In the thirty-five Borough Courts of First Instance, three judges are needed in civil cases, and in criminal cases, as in the rural courts, only one.

Next in the hierarchy are the six Courts of Appeal, on each of which sit four judges. These civil and criminal courts of second instance will hear any appeal, irrespective of a case's gravity.

Finally, there is the King's Supreme Court (*Högsta Domstolen*), with its three divisions and twenty-four justices. It deals only with matters of some public consequence.

Cases of administrative law and procedure have their own tribunals. The highest court of appeal here is the Supreme Administrative Court (*Regeringsrätten*). There is also a special court, the Labour Court, for disputed interpretations of those collective labour agreements which are so vital to Sweden's prosperity and labour peace. It will be considered under that head.

SWEDISH LAW

Swedish law today is a striking blend of traditional and radical qualities. The traditional aspect lies in its administration and basic principles, the radicalism in its content. Basically, Swedish law goes back to old Germanic law, with its emphasis on the individual's rights and liberties. Only in a secondary way has it been influenced by Roman law or, more recently, by Anglo-Saxon ideas of jurisprudence. But the Swedes, as a nation, have absolutely no reverence for antiquity as such. Indeed they are apt to be suspicious of it. During recent decades virtually no aspect of Swedish law has not been closely reconsidered and often profoundly revised in the light of modern circumstances.

These reforms have been made easier because, unlike the British, the Swedes rely largely on a body of written laws—which anyone can look up in a fairly compendious law book. True, there is also a body of case law but this is not legally binding. Instead, the judges have a great deal of discretion in administering statute law, and are often guided less by the letter of the statute, which—from a literary point of view—is often admirably concise and does not therefore attempt to cover all possible circumstances—than by ministerial comments appended to it. This is known as the principle of the "spirit of the legislator" (*lagstiftarens anda*).

Next to the sanctity of the individual, his rights and liberties, Swedish law seeks to protect the sanctity of property and the right of free contract. In practice, of course, socialist legislation has nibbled at the edges of these rights—for example by rent controls, planning, etc—but even after thirty years of Social Democratic government and welfare policies the basic principle of freedom of contract remains unchanged and is subscribed to by all parties.

A final interesting characteristic of Swedish law is that, since the 1870s, more and more of it has been designed in close collaboration with Sweden's Scandinavian neighbours. To bring about such collaboration is one of the prime functions of the Nordic Council, an intergovernmental organ which meets regularly at ministerial level. To a very great extent all five countries' laws have been brought into line, each country in this way profiting by its neighbours' experience. Once again, it has been the purely traditional factor which, by subjecting everything to objective and rational scrutiny, has been sharply reduced. "The law is a piece of social machinery, not a temple."

To become a lawyer (*advokat*) and a member of the Association of Swedish Lawyers (*Advokatsamfundet*) which, like the Inns of Court in Britain is largely self-regulating, it is necessary to be a Swedish citizen, to be at least twenty-five years of age, to have passed the lower law degree (*jur. kand.*), and to have at least five years' practical experience of the law, three of them while working for a lawyer.

POLICE

The duty of prosecuting criminals falls on a distinct office, that of the Chief Prosecutor of the Realm (*Riksåklagaren*), and on his regional and local counterparts. In serious cases the accused is entitled to free legal aid.

Up to 1965 the Swedish police were strongly regionalised and responsible to local government. Since the reform then carried out—a change made in view of the changing structure of society, for instance the shrinking distances of the automobile age— the police force has been a single State organisation.

The highest police official is the *Rikspolischefen*. He is immediately responsible to the State Police Board, on which he sits as a member. The Board has a director-general and five lay members, appointed by the Riksdag, of which they are usually members. As they represent all parties, the Riksdag thus has direct insight into the activities of the police.

Though the police is organisationally a self-contained force, immediate routine authority is normally vested in the county council (*Länsstyrelse*), and each county has its own police chief.

There is a further sub-division into districts, each with its own chief of police. The county traffic police, operating on high-powered motorcycles and helicopters in summer and in cars in winter, both equipped with long-range radios capable of reaching for several hundred miles, constitutes a special reserve force for emergencies. Like the rest of the Swedish police, they are armed with pistols but (as one officer told the author) "we have to be almost dead ourselves before we're permitted to shoot."

The State Police Board also includes a special Criminal Investigation Department (*Rikskriminalen*) whose duty it is to aid the local police in difficult matters and to intervene in such nation-wide dangers as the narcotic traffic, recently a worse plague in Sweden than in many other countries. The *Rikskriminalen* consists of forty highly-qualified policemen, and has its regional equivalents. It is aided by an independent research unit, the State Criminological Laboratory, in Stockholm. Lastly, there is a Security Branch, immediately responsible to the State Police Board. Altogether there are 500 police stations throughout the country, concentrated in 119 places.

PRISONS AND CARE OF OFFENDERS

As in most other countries, the penalties the law imposes are either fines or imprisonment. The death penalty, except for treason in time of war, was abolished in 1921 and no one had been executed for a good many years before that. First offenders are nearly always put on probation, and the law is generally extremely lenient. Even where an offender is sent to prison, the theory is that he is sent there *as* a punishment, but not *for* punishment. An old principle of Swedish law dating back to Renaissance times was that its aim was to reform, not to punish —in the intermediate centuries this was more honoured in the breach than the observance, but today it really does prevail. Psychiatric treatment is often prescribed, and many crimes which in Britain or the USA would be harshly punished are apt to be

written off as mere aberrations. Certain classes of offence are not
viewed by the Swedish law as crime. Youths under eighteen
years of age are not brought before a court at all, but are
committed to the child welfare authorities.

The same humane, non-moralistic attitude is reflected in
Sweden's prisons which, by comparison with most European
or American prisons, are almost homes from home. Just how
liberal they are can be inferred from the type of complaints
brought before the ombudsman by their inmates : petitions that
a prisoner has not been allowed full privacy when visited by wife
or sweetheart; has not been given his regular furloughs (if in an
open prison); or has suffered from too great a diet of TV and
wants more film shows instead. The type of punishment meted
out to drivers found by the police to be under the influence of
alcohol is probably excellent for such persons' health—a spell of
wood-cutting in the forest.

Prisons are under the authority of an autonomous public-
service agency—the National Correction Administration. They
are highly differentiated. Open institutions outnumber the closed,
though the latter have much greater overall capacity. The motto
when building new prisons nowadays is "build the workshops
first, and the prison afterwards." Such prisons as Tillberga, where
120 inmates live what can only be called a normal life, are
fully comparable with any ultra-modern Swedish factory. In
another prison, near the university town of Uppsala, persons
with scholastic aptitude can simply continue their education.

An interesting, and surely very rational, feature of the
Swedish correction system is the "day fine." Instead of levying
an arbitrary sum, laid down by law—arbitrary, that is, in
relation to a convicted person's earning ability—for all minor
offences a court will usually levy a fine of so many "days"
(*dagsböter*). The offender is obliged to pay the equivalent of so
many days' income. Thus, for one and the same offence, a rich
or highly-salaried person will automatically pay perhaps four
or five times what is demanded of someone less well off. Nor is
it difficult to determine the amount in question. The taxation
authorities know all about that, the larger incomes being

published annually, for all to see, in an almanac (*Taxerings-kalendern*).

Young offenders

In Sweden the age of criminal responsibility was fixed long ago at fifteen years. Offenders under this age do not come under the jurisdiction of the courts, but are the responsibility of the child welfare boards. An offender who is already fifteen when he commits his crime may, in principle, be brought before a court and sentenced under the criminal code.

The age group from fifteen to seventeen, inclusive, has long occupied a special position in Swedish jurisprudence, and there is reluctance to deprive them of their liberty. Generally speaking, the category committed to social care comprises the more passive and parasitical youths, those leading disorderly, indolent or immoral lives in which criminal acts play a subordinate role. The correctional system, on the other hand, takes the more actively criminal youths under its charge. Although the code does provide for it, imprisonment may be considered only when "compelling reasons" are present; under no circumstances, moreover, is a life sentence meted out.

———

The electrified ore line from Kiruna in Lapland to Narvik in Norway, the world's most northerly railway.

The school at Eriksdal, Skövde, Västergötland. Catering for children aged 7-15 years, it has thirty-two classrooms; average cost was £10,000 ($26,000) per classroom.

FOREIGN POLICY AND DEFENCE

Since 1814, when a nominal number of Swedish soldiers were in the allied forces which, commanded by the Swedish Crown Prince (the former French Marshal Bernadotte), defeated Napoleon at the Battle of Leipzig, Sweden has not taken part in a war. Her policy of neutrality has so far had striking success. Neutrality, however—as the other Scandinavian countries discovered to their cost in 1940—is not its own guarantee. It is a function of the international balance of power, and of a strong defence.

To some extent Sweden's neutrality is dictated by consideration for Finland's special position. Although involved in a "special relationship" with the USSR, Finland's independence is in Sweden's eyes a condition of Sweden's own security. It was chiefly for this reason that Sweden did not join the Atlantic Pact. Had she done so, the Swedes argued, the Russians might have felt justified under their treaty with the Finns in occupying Finland or in some other way limiting that country's freedom of action.

Most of the great rivers of Northern Sweden have been harnessed to produce hydro-electricity.

In the Volvo factory, Gothenburg. Few jobs are regarded in Sweden as unsuitable for women.

Swedish neutrality, described as a policy of non-alignment, is, however, qualified by the express declaration that the country belongs historically, culturally and in her political institutions, to the west. That is to say, Swedish neutrality is political, not ideological. Sweden is also in favour of all measures to increase the authority of the United Nations, and is always ready to supply mediators, the most famous being the late Secretary General, Dag Hammarskjöld, son of a former Swedish prime minister. So far, Sweden has put 11,000 volunteers at the UN's disposal for peace-keeping missions in Korea, Cyprus, the Congo and other places. The UN mediator in the Israeli-Arab conflict, Gunnar Jarring, is a Swede. Sweden has also played an important role in the Geneva disarmament negotiations, whose chief fruit has been the test ban on nuclear weapons among the great powers. All such matters rate very high in the Swedish newspaper headlines; and it can safely be said that the Swedes, particularly in recent years, are more conscious of such things than most people and even more international in their outlook. At the same time, they are probably apt to over-estimate the importance of their own government's say in international affairs; to regard themselves as the conscience of the world.

Yet they are far from blue-eyed. They realise that their interests are served, first and foremost, by keeping Scandinavia a low-tension area in the world's affairs. This can only be achieved if they themselves have a strong defence. Neutrality imposes on Sweden a disproportionately high burden of expense for weapons. Whereas Norway and Denmark, both in NATO, spend twenty per cent of their defence budgets on purchases of weapons and equipment (hitherto from the USA and Britain, but from 1969 on, largely from Sweden), Sweden has to spend forty per cent. In the budget year 1968-69 about 13.8 per cent of the national budget, or Sw. cr. 5,331 million, (£426 million, $1,066 million) went on defence.

The country's defence, conceived as a whole, has two goals: first, to render any attack on Sweden so expensive a business for an aggressor that the cost of occupying Swedish territory would far outstrip any strategic gains which might accrue;

second, by organising the country for instant conversion to a wartime economy, to keep it running in time of war. In two world wars, Swedes have had to endure blockades. Sweden being dependent both on exports and also on certain vital imports— notably oil and petrol—these blockades proved extremely troublesome, and in World War I led almost to starvation. Should a third occasion ever arise, the Swedish nation hopes to find itself better prepared.

Unlike countries with mass populations and dense urban concentrations, Sweden is favourably situated for self-defence. It should be possible to evacuate about 2.8 million people from the urban areas at very short notice, and a further half-million from certain particularly exposed areas. Such evacuation would be permanent for the duration of the war. Further, the bedrock on which most of the cities and the country as a whole repose offers excellent material against nuclear attack. Vast deep shelters have been blasted out of the rock. Used in peacetime as garages, sports halls, etc, in an emergency they are intended to shelter all that part of the population which would have to remain behind in order to operate the country's defence and vital industries. All houses in urban areas are required by law to have conventional shelters, and in the hallway of every Swedish apartment building evacuation instructions are posted up for its occupants.

The chief sources of the country's industrial power and lighting—the great Norrland hydro-electric power stations—are also deep down in the rock, inaccessible to bombing. The power grid is designed to carry on, even if some of its links should be broken by enemy action. Against the danger of blockade, astonishing stores of foodstuffs and fuels have been assembled. All importers of certain basic materials are required to stock-pile in a ratio of ten per cent against an emergency, and petrol and oil is stored in huge plastic bags, sunk in the lakes.

THE ARMED FORCES

The king is nominally commander-in-chief of the armed forces. The whole country is divided into military commands, each supposedly capable of operating independently should the central government be put out of action.

All Swedish men are conscripted for thirteen months. Called up at the age of 19-20, they undergo a basic course, and thereafter, up to the age of 47, are liable to be called up for 15- to 40-day refresher courses. About 80 per cent of all officers are conscripts, and undergo a 23-month training. On mobilisation, the total strength of the armed forces would be about 650,000 men, but only 22,000 regular officers and NCOs are employed full time in peacetime, together with some 10,000 civilian personnel working for the Air Force. More than 50,000 conscripts are enrolled every year. Further, every able-bodied citizen between the ages of 16 and 65 is liable to serve in civil defence, and voluntary defence organisations have about one million members, of whom 350,000 are women. Conscientious objectors are not forced to bear arms, but on pain of imprisonment must train for non-combatant duties. There is also a Home Guard, which is intended to take the first brunt of local attacks.

In all three arms the weaponry is of the highest quality. Sweden, indeed, is an exporter of combat aircraft from the SAAB factory, and of guns from Bofors AB, in Värmland, manufacturers of the famous Bofors gun of World War II. A certain number of weapons, tanks for instance, are of foreign (notably British) provenance. But the bulk of Sweden's arms are manufactured in Sweden.

The Army aims at quick mobilisation, and its units are trained to operate exclusively in, and be familiar with, the peculiar Swedish terrain and climatic conditions. In addition to its more modern weapons, the old push-bike is still found to come in handy. A great deal of the army's defensive effort would probably have to be deployed in the Arctic, where Sweden joins the

European land-mass. The fortress of Boden, in Lapland, is one of the most military cities in the country.

Nucleus of the army, when mobilised, the armoured and infantry brigades, each have a strength of 5,000 to 6,000 men. British Centurion tanks are used, also the Swedish strv-S (turretless) tank. Anti-tank weapons include the SS-11, Bantam, Carl Gustav, and Miniman. One battalion is equipped with Hawk surface-to-air missiles.

The Air Force is the third strongest in Western Europe. With a total strength of 24,000, including 6,000 regulars and 10,000 civilians, it operates 650 combat aircraft, all of an essentially defensive type. The SAAB J35 *Draken* (Dragon) is an all-weather fighter. The SAAB J32-B *Lansen* (Lance) is to be replaced by the 37 *Viggen* (Thunderbolt), of which 175 are to be delivered in 1971. Altogether there are 43 squadrons: 10 attack squadrons with A-32A Lansen (with air-to-ship missiles), 16 all-weather fighter squadrons with J35 Draken fighters, 6 all-weather fighter squadrons with J32-B Lansen fighters, 5 reconnaissance day-fighter squadrons with S-32 and S-35 planes, and 6 squadrons with Bloodhound 2 surface-to-air missiles. A fully computerised and semi-automatic control and air surveillance system, by which all components of the Swedish air force are co-ordinated, is now operating. This is known as Stril 60, and is similar to the American SAGE.

Pilots undergo special training in using strips of country road for landing and take-off in the event of air bases being destroyed by enemy action.

The Navy consists entirely of light units. Its function is to protect Swedish shipping in time of war, and co-ordinate with the other arms to interfere with, and as far as possible prevent, invasion of Swedish territory.

It is divided into two branches: the naval forces proper, and the coastal artillery. The former consist of some 20 destroyers, 9 fast anti-submarine frigates, 37 torpedo boats, 23 submarines, 1 fleet minelayer, 40 minesweepers and one light cruiser. Two of the destroyers are equipped with Rb-308 ship-to-surface missiles, and two others with Seacat surface-to-air missiles. The coastal artillery consists of a large number of batteries, and Vertol and Alouette naval helicopters. Naval personnel totals 4,600 regulars and 7,000 conscripts.

Not being intended for use outside Sweden's own coastal waters, the navy is specially trained to exploit the archipelagos. Several of its bases are wholly underground and inaccessible to nuclear or other air attack.

It may legitimately be asked how people who have not experienced war for 160 years, and whose values are so essentially peaceable, would react in reality if attacked? Public opinion polls show that, though peaceful, the majority of Swedes are not pacifist. They are well aware that they are living in a dangerous world, and, indeed, in the last two decades, seem to have become more and more so. Intense emotional engagement in the Vietnam war on the part of the younger generation has at times made the government swerve a little from what the American press, at least, considers a strict neutralist position. In 1968, one cabinet minister even went so far as to join in a pro-North Vietnam demonstration, with alarming effects on Sweden's relations with the USA. On the other hand, the Russian invasion of Czechoslovakia in the summer of 1968 produced in Swedes not only a whole-hearted feeling of sympathy for the Czechs —another small nation—but also a measurable drop in their belief in their own capacity to defend themselves in a like situation. After the crisis was over they seemed to recover self-confidence.

One can get the impression that Sweden, for all her high degree of organisational preparedness, might be psychologically unprepared for the realities of a sudden attack. But, given a short time to adapt themselves, the Swedes would probably defend themselves as fiercely as any other nation. The plain fact should be added that Russia is the only country which they can imagine having to defend their country against.

CURRENCY AND TAXATION

The basic currency unit is the *krona*, or Swedish crown, (written SKr. or Sw. cr. pl. *kronor*) it is subdivided into 100 *öre*. The present value of the Swedish krona (considerably higher than the Danish or Norwegian *krone*) is in British money, 1s 8d, and in American, 20c. That is to say, about Sw. cr. 12.55=£1, and Sw. cr. 5=$1. Though 5-kronor pieces are issued, they are not common, nor are the 2-kronor pieces, some of which are still in circulation. The 1-krona piece is therefore the largest "silver" coin, the 50 öre piece the next largest, 25 öre and 10 öre being smaller; the 5, 2 and 1 öre pieces are copper. Banknotes are issued for Sw. cr. 5, 10, 50, 100, 1,000 and 10,000. Only in recent years has the cheque made itself generally acceptable as a method of payment for smaller sums, and it is surprising what large sums of money a Swede will carry about him in cash. On the other hand, a great many payments are made through the Postgiro system, recently imitated in Britain, which has existed in Sweden for thirty years and more. The system may be a convenience to the public, but it does not pay for itself, and has to be subsidised out of postal charges.

The Swede is certainly the world's most highly taxed citizen. For this he has to thank his commitment to his famous welfare state, which affects his life at every juncture, and whose many ramifications will be considered in the next chapter. One factor which has greatly increased the burden of taxation has been that income-tax scales have been little revised since before the war. Being steeply progressive, and the value of money today being only one-quarter of what it then was, everyone is paying taxes which in pre-war days were only paid by the upper income brackets. Thus it is by no means uncommon to pay nearly 50 per cent of one's earnings in direct taxes alone. On the other hand there is an upper limit (80 per cent of assessed income) to the amount of tax any individual can be obliged to pay.

A feature of the system which has just been abolished, and

which, in a country where so many women work, was felt to be particularly invidious, was the joint taxation of man and wife (*sambeskattning*). Until this change was made (1969) it was a standing joke that people couldn't afford to remain married and that they would have to divorce to be able to pay their taxes.

Income tax is not the only direct tax a Swede is liable to pay. There is also a tax on fortunes exceeding Sw. cr. 100,000 (£8,000, $20,000) and a capital gains tax, which, assessed as part of income tax, includes profits from all sales of property, even the taxpayer's own dwelling. The tax on fortunes includes such objects as jewellery, furs, antiques, etc.

In principle the Social Democrats have always opposed indirect taxation; but, as from 1 January 1969, the universal purchase tax hitherto levied on all articles—even books, magazines and newspapers—has been turned into a ten per cent value-added tax (*Mervärdesomsättningsskatt*), known for short as MOMS. Only housing, medical drugs, post office and telephone charges and passenger transport are exempt from MOMS, which covers more than 80 per cent of all goods and services, including hotel room prices and meals in restaurants. It is reckoned at ten per cent of the value of any article or service at each stage of its manufacture, and includes previous tax at earlier stages. Similar systems are in force in France, Western Germany, Holland and Denmark.

RELIGION

From having been a country where the State Lutheran Church exercised a virtual dictatorship over souls, Sweden, as part of her rapid conversion into an industrialised urban society, has become singularly secularised, perhaps more so, and more thoroughly so, than any other western European country.

Nominally, all Swedes are born into the State Lutheran Church, whose 2,500 parishes cover the country, and whose archiepiscopal see is at Uppsala. Well over 90 per cent of all Swedish citizens are still baptised, married and buried in church.

But otherwise, except for the first Sunday in Advent, Christmas and Easter, church attendance is notably low. Though one church authority claims that a quarter of the adult population go to church once a month, a 1966 study in a Stockholm surburb suggests that the correct figure cannot be higher than nine per cent. Of those interviewed, 68 per cent declared that they "had a religion," and 64 per cent said it was Christianity; but only 14 per cent believed the church's dogmas. Twenty-eight per cent had to be classified by the interviewers as deists, and 43 per cent as agnostics.

In striking contrast to their emptiness on Sundays, Swedish churches are pleasing in their invariably aesthetic décor—they have nothing of the shabby seediness of churches in southern lands where religion itself more obviously flourishes. Being State institutions, they are also wealthy, and spend great sums annually on such things as splendid neo-classical (baroque) organs and their own restoration.

Although he cannot help being born into the Church of his forefathers, a Swede is quite free—in conformity with the United Nations clause on freedom of religion—to contract out of it. All he, or she, has to do is to write to the clergyman of the parish and inform him that he has lost a parishioner. This relieves the citizen of his contribution to church tax. But almost no one bothers to secede.

The State Lutheran Church undoubtedly has a heavy air of establishment about it. At present all bishops are appointed by the Minister for Education and Ecclesiastical Affairs—the most recent of whom was an avowed atheist. Its past record of authoritarianism is no doubt its chief enemy, and its prime curse the highly official status and many small bureaucratic duties of its clergy—for instance the keeping of census records. Its disestablishment is very much on the agenda, though the problems attending it are considerable. Some of the clergy are themselves strongly of the opinion that only such a divorce can revitalise the Church. But a recent (1969) *utredning* which, as always, consulted a great number of authorities of all sorts, including the free churches, found there was a majority opinion against disestablishment. For a convinced radical the Swede is in some respects remarkably conservative.

If the State Church is coolly bureaucratic, and the cities strongly secularised, religion still flourishes in a small way in more out-of-the-way rural districts, such as Bohuslän, on the west coast, where the fishermen practise a very dour and puritanical version of Lutheranism known as Schartauism. There are also a number of nonconformist churches, of which the largest is the highly emotional and revivalist "Philadelphia Congregation." The Philadelphians are most critical of the State church and indeed of most other things in modern Sweden. All other non-conformist churches (*frikyrkor*) seem to be steadily losing ground. The Missionary Union (*Missionsförbundet*) numbers about 93,000 members, and the Pentecostal congregations about 91,000. The Methodists have about 10,000 members and the Baptists 29,000. Altogether the "free" churches number some 350,000 adherents. Most of these, it should be noted, also belong nominally to the State Church.

The only church in Sweden which, in a small way, is going from strength to strength is the Roman Catholic. Of its total membership of some 33,000 souls, only 8,000 are Swedes by birth, the remainder being Poles, Italians and other immigrants and foreign residents. Catholicism's chief protagonists are among the intellectuals. Up to quite recent times Catholicism was held in strong abhorrence in Sweden, and this neo-Catholicism among convert writers and intellectuals is new and shocks many people. On the other hand, the intellectual liberalism of these Swedish neo-Catholics in such matters as "the pill" and the over-population of the earth is something of an embarrassment to the Holy See. Clearly, one does not shed one's Swedish skin by becoming a Roman Catholic.

3

How They Live

IN A country with so long and cold a winter a decent home is basic to everyone's existence, and the new Sweden is of course famous for the standard and modernity of its homes. Even if the average, 2½ rooms, 667 sq ft, is on the small side by British or American standards, the Swedish worker's up-to-date flat strikes other Europeans as being in the luxury class. Immaculate plastic-treated parquet floors, central heating, double-glazed windows, electric stove and refrigerator, are all part of the fittings. Three out of every four households in all income classes now have TV, and every fourth household, notwithstanding the communal laundry arrangements usually available in most apartment blocks, has both its own deep-freeze and its washing machine. Amenities tend, of course, to be better in urban than in rural areas.

The Swedes are preponderantly (55½ per cent) a nation of flat-dwellers. But 34 per cent own their own dwelling in a one- or two-family house, and according to a recent Gallup poll, (1968), 52 per cent of the population, given the chance, would like to live in a villa. Nevertheless, it is cheaper to rent an apartment than to live any other way.

The disadvantages of flat life, made necessary by the high cost of construction, are to some extent offset by the prevalence of the *sommarstuga*. There are, at present, nearly half a million of these little summer houses, out in the archipelago, by the shores of some lake or in the countryside. And sixteen per cent of all Swedish families own one. Many deserted farm houses are being converted into summer homes for city dwellers; while for those who cannot afford to own their summer house, holiday villages of summer châlets are going up all over the country. Many large firms have their own holiday areas, and let *sommarstugor* to their employees at nominal rents.

If the Swedish home, however well appointed, seems on the small side, one must bear in mind that it used to be very much smaller. In the early 1930s, 62 per cent of all families were living in grossly crowded conditions, more than two persons per room. In 1933, 40 per cent of large families (three or more children) in the towns were living in one room and kitchen, at a maximum. By 1954 the figure for such overcrowding had dropped to 22 per cent and by 1960 had virtually disappeared (1-2 per cent). Today, the standard 2½-room flat of 667 sq ft is regarded as being too cramped for a family with two children, and the goal is to achieve an average of three rooms and kitchen with a total floor-space of 775 sq ft in the near future. At present, a 3-room apartment, newly-built, costs about Sw. cr. 3,500 (£280, $700) a year in rent, perhaps 20 per cent of its occupier's income after tax. Many categories, furthermore, notably old people and families with many children, can claim housing subsidies, over and above those which, in the form of low-interest loans and mortgages from State or commune, have already gone into their dwellings.

The real rise in housing standards over the past thirty years is best indicated by the fact that an industrial worker today does not have to pay a larger fraction of his salary or wages in rent for a newly-built three-room flat than he would have had to pay for a one-roomer in the early thirties.

The tightly-controlled policies which have brought about this rise in standards have also, however, contributed to a serious housing shortage; a shortage which, in Stockholm particularly, is chronic. No one, of course, is left literally without a roof over his head—though even that was not uncommon in the Stockholm of a century ago; but the demand, especially for higher-grade and larger apartments, greatly outstrips the supply. There is a flourishing black market for those prepared to pay several thousand kronor in key money. But ten per cent of the capital's population is always queueing for newer, larger, or better accommodation, and among their thousands are cases of real hardship. This old-established housing shortage does not look like disappearing in the near future. It is not helped by controlled rents—though rent controls are now progressively being dismantled—nor by the fact that 28 per cent of all new flats being built still have only one room and kitchen. In fact, 50 per cent of those in the housing queue do want a one-roomer: a higher proportion of Swedes than of any other people on earth live alone.

Nor is the housing shortage due to inertia or a slow construction rate, as the government's political opponents would like to make out. Rather, it is a result of sharply-rising standards of living, of acute competition from other consumer goods, notably cars, and also of the extraordinarily high cost of construction. The Swedish building worker—who constitutes 9 per cent of the labour force—earns between 20 per cent and 25 per cent more than any other worker (Sw. cr. 24,000 p.a., £2,000, $4,800) as against the national average of about Sw.cr. 20,000 (£1,600, $4,000). There is also a vast amount of time wasted by the building industry—a recent study in depth showed that housing construction could be made 30 per cent cheaper if all workers in fact worked all the time they are being paid for. In the most efficient firm of all those studied, they were only working 65 per cent of their time! Nevertheless, in 1966 19.2 per cent of gross investments or 8.7 per cent of the gross national product, went into housing construction, resulting in 89,361 new dwellings, the construction rate for the previous year being 12.5 per thousand inhabitants (cf France 8.4 per cent, Britain 7.3 per cent, West Germany 10 per cent and the USSR 9.5 per cent). In 1967 the figure rose to 98,000 new dwellings. Two-thirds of all living units in the cities have been built since the war. Only about 5 per cent date from before 1880.

Nor is the housing shortage helped by the dramatic demolition rate. Sweden never had anything corresponding with British slum conditions, but some of the older parts of the cities are

distinctly forbidding and are rapidly being swept away. There
is also a wholesale destruction of housing which, in the opinion
of its occupants, is still perfectly habitable, and whose demolition
is certainly not justified by any lack of fresh building space.
Huge areas of virgin land all round the cities are still
unexploited. These buildings are just being bulldozed to
make room for more profitable and less spacious modern
blocks.

If the Swedish home is remarkable, it is in its efficiency—the
result of carefully-applied standardisation. Construction has been
made as cheap as is consistent with high and rigorous building
standards, and the dwelling unit is designed to be as easily-
run as possible. A prime example is the Swedish kitchen—
known throughout Germany, from the enthusiastic reports
brought home by tens of thousands of *au pair* girls, as *"die
Schwedenküche."* By measuring and analysing a housewife's
movements about her domain in the course of a 24-hour day,
and given certain standardised limits and overall dimensions,
the optimum disposition of a kitchen can be computed, and
kitchens are constructed accordingly. Most of the said housewife's
movements can simply be eliminated.

Garbage disposal is another example. All dwellings have a
sopnedkast (garbage-disposal hatch), through which wrapped
rubbish is thrown into a central funnel, reaching from the top
of the house to bins at the bottom. At villas and private houses,
the garbage man supplies each (standard) bin with a strong bag
of kraft paper, which obviates both unsightly litter, and the
necessity of lifting heavy bins. Garbage disposal in Sweden is at
least not a sub-human occupation.

Standardisation is also rigidly applied to office buildings, which
are constructed on the module principle, one module being
the minimum cube of space in which an office worker can feel
comfortable and work happily. Superior officials and company
employees have two or three modules, according to rank. On
paper this may seem a horrifyingly beehive approach; in practice,
where the offices are in other respects well-designed, it makes
for working conditions far superior to those often found in a

large London or New York office, which, to the eyes of a Swede, appear horrific rather than quaint.

The great revolution

The revolution in housing, as in so many other aspects of Swedish life, began in the twenties and thirties. The ideas launched in the twenties in Germany under the slogan "sun, air, light," nipped in the bud by the Nazis, took root in Social-Democratic Sweden. In the pre-war era and the forties Sweden was regarded as leading the world in the boldness of her housing projects. Names like Sven Markelius, the Stockholm city architect, swiftly achieved international fame for such projects as his *Gärdet* scheme, on the northern outskirts of the capital. Even, today, they seem refreshingly modern, though Swedes, whose ideal of up-to-dateness is extreme, would probably now regard them as becoming antiquated.

These experiments celebrated their triumphs, but also had shortcomings which led to revaluations. Fortunately, the field was wide open for these; not only was the standard of living rising, but the open ground was available to build on. As early as 1904 a Conservative majority in the Stockholm City Council had far-sightedly acquired all the land surrounding the town, which in those days was much smaller than it is now. By a system of leasehold, prices of building land could be kept under effective control. This policy has paid off handsomely.

Much of the new development originated in competitions, with prizes offered by the city authorities for the planning of whole estates and individual types of houses and blocks. Unfortunately, there was a tendency to begin with the latter and work outwards, with the result that dwellings attractive enough in themselves were often strung out in long strip-like "lamellas" which, on a cold winter's day, produce a singularly dreary and monotonous impression. In 1940 the first landscaping schemes, incorporating tracts of farmland, were launched, and the general principle of introversion in area planning was introduced. Vehicular and pedestrian traffic also began to be separated;

the neighbourhood principle was now being more closely considered.

The *punkthus*—tower block—which has since spread all over the world, was a Swedish invention of the thirties. The topography around most Swedish cities, notably Stockholm, is rather rugged, and clusters of such tower blocks, built in neighbourhoods, stand upon knolls and cliffs against the skyline. The fifties were the era of the tall building. The three-storey blocks, which at the end of the 1940s contained about two-thirds of all new flats, were reduced until they represented only 40 per cent of dwellings, while the proportion of five-to-eight-storey blocks rose from 8 per cent to 20 per cent, and blocks of more than nine storeys from 0.5 per cent to 17 per cent.

Perhaps partly because of this emphasis on height, the neighbourhood system did not quite work out, either. The integration of man with his surroundings, dreamed of by Lewis Mumford in his *Culture of Cities*—a book widely read in Sweden after being translated in 1942—proved unfeasible on this basis.

Another new type of building which proliferated in the postwar period was the "star house." Basically designed as a three-armed shape, with a staircase in the middle and three apartments having front-and-rear exposures on each floor, such structures, joined together, achieved a certain intimacy of atmosphere. Unfortunately the method has proved too expensive, and has since been abandoned.

The sixties were to be the age of the satellite towns. Two dominant considerations have presided over their construction: to protect the human inhabitants from the tyranny of the automobile; and to produce service areas where all the amenities of life, including places of work, should be available. The results have been such famous satellite towns as Vällingby (1956) and Farsta (1960), and latterly Skärholmen (1968), all just outside Stockholm. Vällingby, designed by the architects Sven Backström and Reil Runius, some twelve miles from the centre of Stockholm, can be reached by the brand-new underground railway in twenty minutes. The underground passes beneath the centre, with adjacent ramps on the same level for lorries to deliver to the stores above. The centre itself comprises stores, shops, banks, post office, health clinics and welfare offices, libraries, a civic auditorium, cinema, restaurants and offices. From the outset, parking places were provided for 600 cars. About 2,000 people work here, and so popular has Vällingby become, as a shopping and residential centre, that the floor space has subsequently had to be doubled.

Like all pioneer projects, Vällingby had its defects, Farsta, completed in 1960 by the same architects, tried to remedy them. Even greater allowance was made for deliveries and services of all sorts, and off-street parking is nearly twice as spacious as at Vällingby. All around the central traffic-free plaza and shops, tower blocks soar up, fourteen or sixteen storeys high, on the slopes of hills. The entire satellite town is centrally heated by a nearby atomic energy plant.

Skärholmen (1968), near the main road south of Stockholm, is an even more ambitious project. If Swedes have severely criticised it, this is no more than a measure of their absorption, as a nation, in everything to do with town-planning. Scandinavia's largest community centre, serving 300,000 people both within its own boundaries and in the neighbourhood, Skärholmen is a whole city of glass and concrete. In an area of 1,722,230 sq ft are 80 shops, 30 banks, restaurants, schools, a church, a hotel for old people and apartment houses. Europe's largest indoor car park takes 4,000 cars. Within the centre proper no cars are allowed. For shoppers with small children there is a central nursery, as well as "parking" spaces for children within some of the individual stores. Costing £32 million, or $80 million, to build, Skärholmen preserves fifty prehistoric graves, in its parks, to remind its occupants that, though their town went up yesterday, in a mere four years, they are living on ground occupied by their Bronze-Age ancestors 4,000 years ago.

Besides such ambitious satellite projects—not only near Stockholm, but also round Gothenburg and Malmö—other Swedish cities can show remarkable developments. The Town Planning Act of 1947 gives the authorities considerable powers. A clear distinction is made between comprehensive planning and detailed

E

plans. The State requires all areas to submit master plans, which, when approved, may afterwards be modified in detail. There are also regional plans, affecting more than one city. There is a threefold hierarchy of units: neighbourhoods (10,000 to 15,000 people), sub-communities (50,000 to 120,000) and the city as such, with its tributary area.

The Swedes have also been enormously energetic in redesigning the centres of their cities. Everywhere the bulldozer's growl is heard. In the centre of Stockholm, when its face-lift is complete, nearly 500 old buildings—many of which would have lasted for at least another 200 years—will have been swept away. A Stockholmer, returning from abroad after a few years, hardly recognises the place. Of the city he grew up in, not more than 300 familiar buildings, including churches, etc, will eventually remain. The first great segment of this re-build, Hötorget—a multi-level shopping centre—is virtually complete. With parking and underground railway in its bowels, Hötorget consists of five great skyscrapers, one faced with burnished copper. Some like it, some don't.

Indoor shopping centres are everywhere becoming more common, and in so cold a climate are justified. At Täby, in the capital's northern outskirts, the centrally-heated market place is designed to serve 150,000 people on its rolling conveyor pavements. Similar shopping centres are found at Luleå, in the Arctic, and outside Gothenburg.

Many countries have ambitious housing and city-centre projects. But in Sweden the whole urban landscape seems to be marked by them. The Swedes are justifiably proud of their radically-reconditioned country. If one could have a glimpse of the primitive conditions of sixty or seventy years ago—conditions which they are apt to refer to as medieval—one would surely sympathise. So utterly novel an environment has, however, created a certain unease of spirit, attributable no doubt to a lack of organic development from the past. No valid judgment can be passed on the vast feat of social engineering until Sweden's new cities have been lived in for half a century or so.

WHAT THE "HAVES" HAVE

UN Statistics 1967:	Sweden	France	UK	USA	USSR	Japan
HOUSING						
Percentage of urban dwellings with 1-2 rooms	25.1	40.0	4.6	7.2	—	33.8
3-4 rooms	52.8	46.8	37.6	33.3	—	39.6
5 rooms or more	22.1	13.2	57.8	59.5	—	26.6
piped water	98.1	89.8	99.5	98.9	—	77.8
bath	80.5	37.3	79.1	96.3	—	51.2
COMMUNICATIONS						
Motor vehicles per 1000 inhabitants	260	224	212	471	—	81
Telegrams per 100 inhabitants	75	49	52	53	118	92
Telephones per 100 inhabitants	46	13	21	50	—	13
Letters per inhabitant	202	173	217	385	23	99
TV sets per 1000/pop.	227	151	253	376	81	192
PRICES						
Rises in consumer prices 1963-1967, per cent	21	12	15	9	—	21
CONSUMPTION						
Daily calorie consumption per inhabitant	2,905	3,250	3,250	3,140	—	2,350
Annual consumption per inhabitant, kgs						
Potatoes	95	101	103	45	—	63
Meat	51	94	74	100	—	10
Milk	234	206	215	240	—	37
Coffee	11.31	4.49	1.21	7.11	0.12	0.18
Tea	0.17	0.04	4.35	0.30	0.26	0.80
Tobacco	1.65	1.69	2.58	4.40	1.17	1.85
Beer, litres	30.71	38.80	89.50	58.50	13.00	16.50
Wine, litres	3.94	128.0	2.11	3.50	4.00	0.40
Liquor, litres	5.0	3.5	1.57	4.66	—	—
Daily newspapers, circulation/1000 pop.	501	245	488	312	274	465
Books, production by number of titles 1965	6,748	23,823	28,789	58,517	72,977	30,451
Cinemas, annual attendance per inhabitant	7	5	5	12	18	4

STANDARDS OF LIVING

Standards of living, as between one country and another, are notoriously difficult to compare. Notwithstanding his small home, the Swede obviously does well. More than one family in three owns its home. Every Swede is entitled to twenty-four days' holiday with pay each year, and many take more; there is one car to every three inhabitants (Britain has one car to every six). Real wages rise steadily at the rate of about four per cent per annum, and so forth. The following table perhaps gives a solid indication of the earning conditions of the industrial worker:

Working a 42-hour week,
it takes him 12 minutes to earn a loaf of bread

27	,,	1 lb of butter
47	,,	1 lb of pork chop
17	,,	1 lb of eggs
38	,,	1 lb of coffee
24	,,	20 cigarettes
36	,,	a cinema ticket
27	,,	1 gallon of gasoline
37	hours to earn	a suit
140	,,	a TV set
30	,,	a bicycle
1,412	,,	a small car

By 1975, at present rates of growth, there will be more cars in proportion to population than currently in the USA, a ratio which planners now take into their calculations. The only challenger to such a standard of living in Europe would perhaps be the Swiss.

Sociologists divide the population into three social (ie income) groups. Group I includes large landowners, industrialists, high-ranking salaried employees of State and industry, altogether about eight per cent of the population. Group II consists of smaller landowners, craftsmen, general salaried employees, salesmen, shopkeepers, etc, and comprises about forty-eight per cent. Group III, what in old terminology used to be called the working class (labourers, lesser service personnel, household employees, etc) includes approximately forty-four per cent. In 1965 the median income for Group I was Sw.cr. 28,000 (£2,200, $5,600) for Group II Sw. cr. 17,000 (£1,360, $3,400) and for Group III Sw. cr. 16,000 (£1,280, $3,200), These figures are based on declarable incomes for income-tax purposes, and are on the low side—it is known that a large part of the population has untaxed earnings on the side. Every other person in Group I earned more than Sw. cr. 34,000 (£2,500, $6,600) but only 1.4 per cent had an income over Sw. cr. 50,000 (£4,000, $10,000), while 35 per cent of the working population had an income of around Sw. cr. 15,000 (£1,200, $3,000) a year. Even allowing for the cost of living in Sweden, and the high rate of taxation—which together make living in Sweden more than twice as costly as in Britain, and as high as, or even higher than in the United States—income-wise, Sweden is an affluent country. Nevertheless, there is certainly a large small-income group, who find it hard to make ends meet on a mere Sw. cr. 15,000 (£1,200, $3,000) a year, or less. On the other hand, one can safely assert that there is no extreme poverty.

In 1967, 41.1 per cent of the GNP (Sw. cr. 129.9 thousand million, £10.3 thousand million, $25.9 billion) went to investments, of which 8 per cent was central government, 7.5 per cent local government, and 8.7 per cent housing. Private consumption accounted for 66.4 per cent, and public consumption for 26.1 per cent. So far, production has managed to keep ahead of consumption; but the MOMS tax, mentioned above, has been introduced largely as a brake on excessive consumption, and as an alternative means of raising taxes without unduly penalising industry.

WHAT THEY EAT AND DRINK

Swedes sometimes wryly concede that "because of their high standard of living, they can't afford to eat." The daily diet can strike a foreigner as somewhat meagre. A cup of coffee and a roll for breakfast, a cup of coffee and an open Scandinavian sandwich—admittedly a sizeable snack in itself—for lunch, followed by yet another cup of coffee in mid-afternoon, and so home to a two-course dinner out of the deep-freeze. In fact the Stockholmer does seem to live largely on coffee and his own ambition; stomach ulcers and nervous breakdowns are by no means reserved for tycoons. On the other hand, in the past twenty years, there has been a total revolution in the quality of the food eaten. Up to quite recent times, lack of green vegetables in wintertime led to a diet of salted and preserved fish, meat, sausage and cheese. Sugar, in a cold climate, was an important ingredient in almost everything, and is still included in most sorts of bread. The typical Swedish meal still begins with *sill och potatis* (sweetened, fresh-water Baltic herring and a boiled potato) with a glass of *snapps* (acquavit), and tails off without any discernible dessert. Favourite everyday dishes are "Jansson's Temptation," an anchovy dish, with potatoes and onions, baked in an oven; *pytt-i-panna*, a hash of meat and potatoes with a fried egg or preferably two; Swedish meatballs, which also contain onions; and thick pea soup with chunks of pork swimming in it, traditionally eaten in most Swedish homes on Thursday. There are numbers of attractive ways of serving up salmon and other fish, and a great array of different sorts of sausage. Meat off the bone is extremely expensive; nowadays, when they can afford it, the Swedes tend to serve it in the French way, an improvement on their traditional over-cooking of sliced beef.

But the most famous of Swedish meals—for it is really a whole meal in itself, even if served only as a huge prelude—is the smörgåsbord. This, in its full glory, can consist of a hundred dishes: salads, salted, smoked and preserved fish and eels of many sorts, salmon, great west coast prawns, many different sorts of cold meat, sausage, cheeses, etc, etc. This magnificent and most elegantly-displayed cold table is still to be experienced in all its amplitude on board the liners of the Swedish American Line and Swedish Lloyd, and in a few tourist hotels at lunchtime, where, for a pound or a couple of dollars, one can sample its delights until one can take no more. Otherwise it is a rarity, or reserved for special occasions like Christmas or Easter.

The correct way to tackle this bewildering array of dishes is to load one's plate first with the fish items, prawns, eels, sardines, anchovies, smoked and "buried" (*gravad*) salmon, etc. Then one comes back for the meats, and finally for the cheeses. Most first-timers, ignorant that all this is no more than a prelude, can only stare aghast, when the entrée subsequently arrives. In the last twenty years there has been a commendable revolution in many other aspects of Swedish cooking; the smörgåsbord needs none.

There has been no equivalent revolution in the Swede's drinking habits. Acquavit, which is distilled from potatoes, has a 67 per cent alcohol content. Since the eighteenth century it has been the Swede's national strong beverage, and at times their national scourge. Its devastating effects finally led to a rationing system—the Bratt System—which lasted for nearly forty years (1922-1958). Today, though rationing has been abolished, wines and spirits are still only sold by the State Wine and Liquor Monopoly (*Systemet*). Efforts have been made to get the Swedes to drink more beer and wine, and less spirits. There are four categories of beer: Class III ("export" or strong beer), Class IIB ("medium beer," *Mellanöl*), Class IIA Pilsener, and finally Class I ("*Lättöl*") which is hardly beer at all. Meanwhile the alcohol problem remains. Misuse of alcohol is thought to be, for instance, the chief reason for divorce.

A Swedish drink which can be quite pleasant after dinner is a liqueur called "*punsch*." Usually it is drunk either warm or ice-cold. Very popular in Strindbergian days, *punsch* has recently been coming into fashion again among young people.

As to coffee, the Swedes are the world's highest per-capita consumers.

A Swede is usually self-conscious about his appearance, and as in other things, he is apt to be something of a perfectionist. A first-time visitor to Sweden is always struck by the absence of anyone, of any class, who is not well-dressed. A group of Swedes at a party or business meeting, or taking a Sunday walk, will look as if they have all come straight from the tailor's. A Swede who is going golfing dresses for the part, to an Anglo-Saxon mind, to the point of caricature. That people of other nations do not always bother so much with their clothes can be regarded by the Swede as a sign of poverty and barbarism. ("Everything that lies south of Denmark we regard as virtually in Africa".) This is all perhaps just a transitory facet of a *nouveau-riche* society.

HOLIDAYS

Of the eleven national holidays, the most important are Christmas, midsummer and Easter. The basic twenty-four days' annual holiday with pay is often taken in two parts: a fortnight in the summer, usually in July, when all industries close down and offices close at 4 pm, and a week in February. Formerly the winter holiday used to be spent in the mountains, skiing. But more and more people get some much-needed winter sunshine by flying south to Majorca or Madeira.

Civil servants have the longest holiday, of forty-days. After reaching the age of 30, any employee of the State or commune has a right to a minimum of 27 days, which at the age of 40 rises to 30 days. In industry, only the highest-ranking employees get 30.

The industrial working week is 42.5 hours. White collar

workers, working a five-day week, do 40 hours. The agreed goal is a universal 40-hour week, but it is a matter of controversy just how soon Sweden can afford to introduce it.

Swedes write and speak much of their "free-time problem." Community centres and holiday villages are springing up everywhere though whether they are in fact the solution to the problem remains to be seen. Also, it is felt that the Swedes, who used to be a notably sports-minded nation, do not take enough exercise, and that the automobile is destroying the nation's physique. There is therefore renewed emphasis on physical fitness. Many hotels run special *motionssemestrat*—physical-fitness holidays.

But perhaps Swedes do not have as much real leisure as their statistics show. Many have secondary occupations on the side—*extraknäck* which bring earnings crucial to their economy. They allege that they cannot afford the leisure the law guarantees them, "if they are to pay their taxes." In certain organisations, for instance the Swedish Broadcasting Corporation, it has been found necessary to enforce regulations preventing employees from working during their holidays and so depriving themselves of necessary relaxation. This preoccupation with work may also belong to the modern Swede's psychological make-up—a built-in part of life in a cold country.

THE WELFARE MACHINE

There is no longer any serious discussion of the welfare state's justification. The most conservative Swedish politician would in this respect no doubt rank as a socialist among British or American colleagues. Where argument still does arise is between the Left, who maintain that the welfare machine needs to be built out still further, and the "bourgeois" parties, who are strongly of the view that it has already gone far enough, and is costing enough, as it is. The national welfare (Social) budget grew from Sw. cr. 1,700 million in 1949, to Sw. cr. 10,500 million in 1966. It is still growing.

Generally speaking, the system covers every aspect of life where an individual may suffer through economic circumstances or from other troubles that he is not qualified to fight single-handed. The system has gaps—there is no national unemployment insurance, and no free dentistry, as in Britain. But with these exceptions it is about as comprehensive as the wit of man can devise.

Before he is even born, a Swedish baby's mother, will, like a British mother, have attended free maternity clinics and had a right to a dental service, three-quarters of the costs of which have been defrayed by the State. She has been able to call on the free services of a district midwife, though virtually all babies, with the exception of the small percentage born in (free) taxis on their way there, are nowadays born in hospital, to have free prophylactic medicines and free participation in ante-natal gymnastic exercises. If she is gainfully employed, the law has guaranteed her six months' leave of absence from her job— no Swedish woman, or any foreign national working in Sweden, may be dismissed from a job on grounds of absence due to child-birth. When her baby is finally born, she receives a cash grant of Sw. cr. 1,080 (£85, $216). If she has given birth to twins or triplets, she receives a further Sw. cr. 540 (£43, $108) per child. A mother who has been earning not less than Sw. cr. 2,600 (£208, $520) a year, and who has been receiving sickness benefit for not less than 270 consecutive days immediately before child-birth or the expected day of delivery, is entitled to a supplementary sickness allowance varying from anything between Sw. cr. 1 and Sw. cr. 46 (£4, $9) a day.

Special help is given to "single parents." The term "illegitimacy" has officially been abolished—no Swedish child comes illegitimate into the world, and the old stigma has in fact largely disappeared. In cases where mother and child constitute what is called a "one-parent family," a child welfare officer is appointed to take care of the child's interests, supervise its up-bringing and help the mother in any way he can. At present there are some 100,000 one-parent families, with about 130,000 under-age children. Of these parents, 11,000 are men. In 1965, there were about 145,000 children under the supervision of some 15,000 welfare officials.

The foreign press has rather luridly publicised the "block of flats for unmarried mothers" in Sweden. A few such *kvinnohus* (women's houses) do in fact exist, though by no means all their occupants are unmarried mothers. But such service flats are all too few, and unmarried mothers in general have to manage much as other mothers do, with the additional problem of earning the greater part of their own and their child's living. Should the father default on his payments, however, the State will advance the sums regularly to the mother, and extract them from the father afterwards. Domestic assistance is almost un-obtainable. In case of illness, the social welfare office may be able to find home helps, home samaritans and children's nurses.

An index-regulated pension, currently Sw. cr. 1,300 (£106, $260) a year, is payable to a child until his sixteenth birthday if one of his parents dies, and Sw. cr. 1,820 (£146, $364) is paid for the loss of both. There are also widows' pensions, but they vary with the widow's age, full pensions only being payable to those over 50 at the death of their spouse (see also Supplementary Pensions below).

As soon as a toddler is old enough for a play-school or day nursery a place can probably be found for him, at any rate within a major city. It is true that nothing like enough such nursery schools and kindergartens exist, and it is hoped that places for 70,000 more children will be ready by 1975. The steady increase in the numbers of gainfully-employed mothers of small children has forced the authorities to give serious attention to the problem.

There are three types of day nursery. The *daghem*, attended each day by 20,000 Swedish children, is open all day for children of pre-school age. About 10,000 go to municipal family day nurseries (*familjedagham*), established in private homes, not subject to the authorities and not subsidised. Finally there are afternoon homes, *fritidshem*, where children can eat, do lessons and occupy themselves when their mother is at work, and *lekskolor* (play-schools) which are attended by 70,000 children daily; the latter are not usually available to the children of gainfully-employed mothers.

From the day he was born, a Swedish child's mother has been receiving a child allowance of Sw. cr. 900 (£73, $174) a year per child. This will not cease until his sixteenth birthday. When he goes to school, all schooling, all schoolbooks, and all necessary dental and psychological attention will be given free, up to and even including university level, when he will be able to apply for various study loans and grants.

When at last he is himself thinking of getting married, the State is at hand to ease the decision; not only with marriage-counselling centres, but with cash loans. Not only newly-married people, but single parents, and even foreigners permanently resident in Sweden, can apply for a home-furnishing loan. The size of the loan, with a maximum of Sw. cr. 5,000 (£400, $1,000), will vary according to the applicant's circumstances; actual need must be proved, and the applicant must be able to show that he or she is industrious and has exercised normal prudence, for example that he has taken out a life-insurance policy.

The Swedish State regards housing of a certain standard as a basic human right. Thus families can apply for housing loans for an apartment or new house, for first or second mortgage real-estate loans (but seventy per cent of the collateral value must be covered by a bank) and for State housing loans which cover a further fifteen per cent of the collateral value, amortisable over a thirty-year period. Loans are also available for the modernising and rebuilding of properties.

More unusual still is the special system of rent allowances for families with children. Up to 1968 the system was that a family which could prove that it was living in an over-crowded dwelling, and could not afford a better one, could apply for a rent subsidy in order to be able to live somewhere more spacious.

The method, as will be imagined, gave rise to anomalies, and was changed from 1969. But the basic principle is that families should not, for economic reasons, be forced to live in sub-standard dwellings.

Similarly, families with very small incomes receive extra allowances on top of the normal *barnbidrag* or basic child allowance. These can amount to Sw. cr. 780 (£64, $156) a year, plus Sw. cr. 230 (£18, $46) for each child under sixteen years of age. Housewives badly in need of a holiday can apply for help to get one. Such grants include both the cost of travel and of the stay at a rest home.

Industrial insurance against injury or disease arising from an employee's occupation is obligatory, and the cost falls on the employer. It is calculated in relation to the employee's normal earnings, including not only what he gets from his job, but also income from any enterprises he may have on the side, such as a farm or private workshop. The value of the housework done in the home is also included in calculating his compensation for injury or industrial disease.

MEDICINE

Even if Sweden does not have Britain's completely free national health service, the situation is very different from that in the USA. All treatment at Swedish hospitals and clinics is free, and so, virtually, is hospitalisation in a public ward. So is all transport by taxi to hospital, even if the journey is a hundred miles, as it can well be in the far north : the costs of such transport are refunded against the driver's receipt. For this and other reasons Swedish taxi-drivers, if requested, will always give receipts. If, on the other hand, a doctor is called to a home, then his fee—which may be quite substantial—must be paid in cash and his receipt obtained. The patient then has the receipt presented at the nearest health insurance office, which will refund about three-quarters of it.

All Swedes over sixteen and foreign residents are entitled

to sickness benefit. Since the contributions are made in connection
with income tax, the benefits are related to income. To qualify
for a basic sick benefit of Sw. cr. 6 a day the contribution, on
average, will be about Sw. cr. 115 (£8.10, $23) a year, supposing
the income from gainful employment to be less than Sw. cr.
2,600 (£208, $520). Such low-income groups would also qualify
for supplementary sickness benefit. In hospital, Sw. cr. 5 per
day is deducted towards the cost of the hospital bed. As long
as earning capacity is reduced by at least half, sickness benefit
is payable for an indefinite period. For old-age pensioners there
is a time-limit of 180 days.

Swedes lament the almost total disappearance of the old
family doctor. Not only has modern medicine become so specialised that, for all practical purposes, he has become an uneconomic anomaly; distances in Sweden make it less rational for
the doctor to come to his patient than for the patient to travel
to a hospital clinic. Unfortunately this method leads to a sort
of mechanisation of doctor-patient relationship. Recent studies
in Swedish hospitals revealed that doctors of the new generation
are so unused to having any personal knowledge of or interest
in their patients that they find it positively embarrassing to have
to talk to them, and therefore take refuge behind a magisterial
manner and their own white coats. In view of the fact that at
least a third of all hospital cases—perhaps of all cases—are really
untreatable except in terms of their psychosomatic origins, it is
being proposed that medical students shall devote much more
of their time to psychological matters. As long, however, as there
is no initial personal relationship between doctor and patient,
and their contact only occurs within the hurried and impersonal
frame of a polyclinic, it is rather doubtful whether so methodical
an approach will solve the alarming pressure of psychosomatic
illness, characteristic of modern society everywhere, and of
Sweden (as a very modern society) in particular. The ratio of
beds in mental hospitals to beds in ordinary hospitals is about
5 to 7.

On the other hand, most people who have ever been treated,
even for the most minor ailments, in a Swedish hospital or

clinic are usually amazed at the thorough approach. Blood tests, metabolic rate tests, electrocardiograms, etc, are routine wherever there can be the least reason for them. All is free. Virtually all Swedish hospitals have automated pathology, still a rarity in Britain, and by no means universal in the USA.

Naturally, it is also possible to go to a private doctor, though highly expensive.

No profession certainly, is more honoured in Sweden than a doctor's. So much is clear not only from public opinion polls ("what would you most like your son to be when he grows up?") but also from the hero-roles played predominantly by handsome young doctors in women's magazines. Though employed in hospitals as a servant of the public, a Swedish doctor also earns a good income, mostly from private practice—albeit not quite so good, perhaps, as that of many a dentist; there is no national dental service. Nevertheless there is a fairly acute shortage of doctors, and a grave shortage of nurses. To become a doctor a Swede first does a two-year course to get his *med. kand.* degree (intermediate MB), and then four and a half years more to get his *med. lic.* (MB), each year comprising ten months of full-time instruction. Finally, his education is usually completed by doing two years in a hospital or scientific institution. Though intake is restricted, the number of doctors has risen rapidly, from about one doctor per 1,000 inhabitants in the fifties to over one per 800 today. Each year sees about 500 new doctors passing their *med. lic.* exam, and by 1975 the number of full-time practising doctors will have risen from today's 10,000 to some 16,000. At the same time there is a considerable intake of foreign doctors; in 1968, 15 per cent of newly-licensed doctors held foreign medical degrees. Such foreign degrees have to be supplemented, however, by special courses, arranged by the State and the medical authorities. The laws against quacks and charlatans are strict.

The shortage of nurses sometimes nullifies the lavish investment in hospital equipment. A dramatic illustration of this occurred when the victims of a road accident, at a spot equidistant from three towns were rushed by ambulance first to one municipal clinic, and then to another, but for lack of staff could not be admitted into any. Two of the patients died. A newspaper, looking into the scandal, found that in point of fact there were plenty of nurses living in all three cities, but that partly because of joint taxation of husband and wife, many had given up their profession as unprofitable, causing whole wards to close down.

It is hoped that the abrogation of the joint income-tax system will remedy this situation. Even so, it is estimated that the combination of increasing illness and a higher geriatric rate will, within a few years, mean that every third Swedish girl leaving school will have to become a nurse, if the situation is not to get wholly out of hand.

PENSIONS

The latest major addition to the Swedish social security system has been a comprehensive National Supplementary Old-Age Pension. Its introduction was fought tooth-and-claw by the opposition parties in the Riksdag, who feared that the vast accumulations of capital which would accrue to the State from the obligatory mass insurance of the whole nation would prejudice the entire money market, and give the government great economic powers independent of taxation-by-representation. The measure was forced through, however, and is so far unique of its kind. It is also probably the world's cheapest pension scheme.

As its name indicates, it supplements the ordinary old-age pension, currently amounting to Sw. cr. 4,585 (£362, $917) a year for a single person, and Sw. cr. 7,150 (£572, $1,430) for a married couple. The idea is to provide every wage-earner, on retirement, with a substantial pension directly related to—in practice about two-thirds of—his or her earnings in his or her prime. There are upper and lower limits to qualifying incomes, that part of the income lying outside these lines not counting for the calculation of supplementary pension. The eligible sum is termed the *pension-bearing income*, and it is a percentage of this amount—at present 2 per cent—which is payable by the employer in premiums. Self-employed persons must pay their own.

For each year that a person has been in receipt of pension-bearing income, he or she is credited with a certain number of pension-points. These are obtained by dividing the pension-bearing income by the "basic amount," which fluctuates with the value of money. A basic amount of Sw. cr. 5,500 (£440, $1,100) and a pension-bearing income of Sw. cr. 9,900 (£790, $1,980) corresponding to an earned income of Sw. cr. 15,400 (£1,232, $3,090), thus yield 1.8 pension points. The basic amount in 1969 stood at Sw. cr. 5,800.

To obtain a full pension it is necessary to have worked for thirty point-bearing years, and amount payable is determined by the pension-points accumulated. If they have been accumulated for more than fifteen years, then the pension is based on the average of the fifteen best years. To calculate the pension, one multiplies the average number of pension points for the 15 best, that is most profitable, years by the "basic amount" for the month in which the pension becomes payable.

It should be noted that, unlike the new British scheme, which appears to be modelled upon it, the Swedish supplementary pension thus contains a built-in guarantee against inflation. If the cost-of-living index rises, then so will the "basic amount," and, therefore, so will all pensions being paid out at that time. If the index falls, so will they. This seems so crucial a dimension —the devaluation of money being always the great bugbear of old age—that the British scheme seems almost intentionally evasive in omitting it.

There are also special safeguards for disabled persons or those who have to retire early—a system called "assumed points"—points not actually earned, but calculated for the years yet remaining, had the pensioner been able to work up to retirement age. Widows and dependent children receive a percentage of the pension—for example, a widow with three children will get seventy per cent.

F

CARE OF THE OLD

If a pensioner is not living in suitable accommodation, he or she can apply for something better in a block of pensioners' flats. At present such flats house about 5 per cent of Sweden's aged population. Some have collective facilities, assembly halls, hobby rooms, restaurants or central kitchens, and medical services—all under one roof. More recently, pensioners' flats have been incorporated in mixed blocks. The State pays special subsidies to builders building such flats.

According to their degree of decrepitude, physical help is given to the old in three forms: first, in their own homes (open care), second, in old people's homes, and third, in hospitals for the chronically ill. But the pressure on the apparatus is tremendous, and however fast it grows, the demand seems to outstrip it. Thus in Gothenburg, a city with just over half a million inhabitants, about 6,000 pensioners are at present receiving help of the first sort from the Social Bureau; at least 2,000 more should be doing so. Of the total, 3,400 are fortunate enough to be living in special pensioners' flats, where the rent is paid either partially or wholly by society. The usual age of admission into old people's homes is too high: eighty years, at least. And although, in theory, everyone in such a home ought to have a room to himself, in reality three- and four-bed rooms are still common. Above all, the labour shortage, together with ever shorter working hours, puts tremendous pressure on the staff, who do not have enough time to take the proper personal interest in the old people. There are 1,630 places available in Gothenburg's old people's homes, and a queue of 2,550 are waiting urgently to come in; while of those who are already in, 400 should really be in hospitals for the chronically ill if the beds were available.

As an ever-greater percentage of the population consists of pensioners—11.5 per cent men, 14 per cent women* the

* Sweden has the highest male geriatric percentage in the world. Cf. USA 8.3 per cent, France, 9.7 per cent, UK 9.6 per cent.

problem of old age is likely to become ever more acute. One thing is clear in Sweden as elsewhere : no automatic solution to it is provided even by a highly prosperous and organised society.

4

How They Work

SWEDEN's economy, the most industrialised in Scandinavia, has emerged unscathed from two world wars. In both post-war periods, therefore, the Swedes have undoubtedly enjoyed great initial advantages. On the other hand, prosperity and a high standard of living bring their problems: notably high labour costs, which must be a considerable headache for any country which, like Sweden, lives by exports. One-fifth of the Swedish gross national product is exported.

The basic principle underlying government policy since World War II has been to maintain full employment. It was on this ticket that the Social Democrats first came into power in the thirties and, by and large, allowing for the usual seasonal fluctuations and one or two minor recessions, they have succeeded. Unemployment since the war has never risen above 1.5 per cent, a very low figure indeed. From 1946 to 1965 the number of persons employed rose on average by 1 per cent per annum, all of which was due to a net increase in immigration. Altogether 170,000 aliens are employed and a further 10,000 immigrate every year. It has also been due to an ever greater reliance on female labour. In 1965, 45 per cent of all married Swedish women in Stockholm were gainfully employed, as against 25 per cent in 1946. Ever since the war it has been people, not work, that have been difficult to find.

The full-employment policy, which economic writers regard as peculiar to Sweden, has implied an acceptance of controlled inflation. By an ever-rising productivity, based on advanced automation, and by fiscal measures, it has been possible to check this. In 1963 the GNP was Sw. cr. 87,040 million (£6,960 million, $17,408 million) which represented an increase of 55 per cent since 1950. During the rest of the 1960s it has grown at a rate of about 4.9 per cent per annum. Full employment has been largely responsible for the unions' lack of resistance to automation.

Another striking feature of industrial policy has been the refusal to featherbed industry. It is a basic Swedish principle that any industry must prove the quality of its products by paying its way in an open market, in competition with goods from other lands. Sweden is an enemy of all trade barriers, and obstinately pursues a low-tariff policy in everything except agriculture.

A Socialist Country?

Sweden has the reputation of being a socialist country. If by this is meant a welfare State, then—as has been seen in the previous chapter—the cap fits. But if by socialism is meant State ownership of the means of production, then she is notably not so. Only 4 per cent of industry is State-owned, and only 7 per cent of the labour force is State-employed. State-owned industries include the iron mines in Lapland (95.7 per cent), the North Bothnian Steelworks, the Scandinavian Airlines System (three-sevenths Swedish, two-sevenths Danish and two-sevenths Norwegian), the State Railways (sj), the Swedish Atomic Energy Co, the Central Restaurant Co (99 per cent), the Swedish Tobacco Co (98.9 per cent), the Wine & Spirits Monopoly (97.3 per cent), the State Lottery and—oddly—the State Football Pool Monopoly (*AB Tipstjänst*), both 100 per cent State-owned. Besides the Bank of Sweden (*Riksbanken*), which issues currency, there are also the State Credit Bank and the Postal Bank (*Postgiro*). The State also has strong holdings in Uddevalla Shipyards (50 per cent), and entirely controls the Airport Administration, the State Power Board and the Swedish Forest Service (*Domänstyrelsen*), though these are not strictly speaking companies.

In the last twenty-five years of "socialist" rule, the only industry to be nationalised has been the Kirunavaara-Luossavaara AB, which operates the Lapland mines on behalf of the State, but this takeover was foreseen from the outset, when the company was established around the turn of the century. Recently, it is true, there has been a slight trend towards greater State participation in industry. Six new companies have been formed, either by the State alone or in co-operation with old-established concerns. In 1967, investments in State-owned companies amounted to Sw. cr. 2,100 million (£88 million, $420 million), or about 12 per cent of total investments in the industrial and business sector.

All the rest of industry is in the private sector; 92 per cent is purely private enterprise, and 4 per cent co-operative-owned. That there is an unusual degree of collaboration and joint forward-planning between the State and the major industrial firms is another matter.

Symptomatic of the "socialist" State's understanding of the practical economics of business and industry is the investment funds system—a tax investment scheme designed to promote a shift of private investment from boom periods to periods of recession. Under this scheme, companies may set aside part of their profits as investment funds, about half the amount being obligatorily deposited with the Bank of Sweden. The funds may then be used for approved investments, or, after a five-year period, without such approval. No tax is levied on them until they are utilised. In practice, a Swedish businessman, or enterprise, can declare as taxable income just as much of the net profits as, taking a long-term view, seems justified. In this way industry has large discretionary control over its own resources, and can save about twenty-five per cent of the cost of buildings financed in this way and about ten per cent of the cost of machinery.

Localisation of industry

The State has also shown enterprise in the localisation of

industry and the re-training of labour. With industry so widely scattered, the close-down of a single factory may put half a community out of work and a mobile labour force is crucial. Less and less dependent on having its sources of power immediately to hand, with the great nuclear thermal power stations and long-distance high-tension cables bringing the electric power from Norrland, industry tends ever more to cluster round its markets and suppliers in central and southern Sweden. This has led to employment problems, above all in Norrland. Investment funds, reserved from taxation under the special arrangement described above, may always be used for developments in this area—which, as we have seen, comprises two-thirds of the country. In the five-year period 1965-70 the State has also lavished Sw. cr. 800 million (£62 million, $160 million) in subsidies there.

Industrial Structure

Late industrialisation helped Sweden to avoid the evils of the paleo-industrial era. Blessed with abundant resources of three basic raw materials—forests, iron ore, and hydro-electric power—she swiftly became the most industrialised country in Scandinavia. But the picture of her economy which emerges today is no longer deeply marked by raw materials. It is a pattern closely resembling that of any other highly industrialised land. This is obvious from her exports. From being predominantly raw materials (timber, pulp, iron ore) around the turn of the century, fifty per cent are today at least finished goods and highly specialised products.

This development is reflected in a traditional and highly characteristic Swedish industrial unit: the *bruk*. In the old days the word *bruk* meant an iron mine, with some farms attached. Today it can mean anything, and probably means several things. Far out in the forests of central and northern Sweden, one comes upon a flourishing industrial centre, owned and operated by a single company whose activities seem to comprise a whole little state in themselves. Very likely mining, for iron ore, phosphates, aluminium etc, is still carried on; but, instead of being exported in crude condition, these products are highly refined and often integrated in the company's many other activities; forestry on a big scale, agriculture, and hydro-electric power. Thus the Stora Kopparberg Company, at Falun, said to be the oldest company in the world, with a charter going back to the fourteenth century, was originally a copper mine.

"Storan" is now a many-sided, highly up-to-date industry, engaged in everything from mining to high-grade steels, forestry and paper-making. When considering Swedish industry branch by branch, it is therefore important to bear in mind that there is often intimate managerial co-ordination of activities at company level.

By international standards, even the largest Swedish firms are only about thirteen per cent the size of their American counterparts. Measured in output and productivity, the comparison is not quite so much to Sweden's disadvantage. Altogether, it is remarkable that Sweden, which has only one four-hundredth of the world's population, answers for a fortieth of its total exports. A mere 37 Swedish manufacturing concerns account for 60 per cent of this amount, and an even smaller group of 10 concerns provide 27 per cent of it. The latter are: ASEA (electrical), AB Götaverken (shipbuilding), LKAB (iron ore), Mo & Domsjö AB (chemicals), Sandvikens Järnverks AB (high-grade steels), Svenska Cellulosa AB (pulp), SKF (ball bearings—"Skefko"), LM Eriksson (telecommunications), Uddeholms AB (steel and other products), and Volvo (cars).

The Great Labour Peace

To an immeasurable extent Sweden's present wealth and prosperity repose upon a basic feeling of co-operation between management and labour. Since lack of such co-operation is the bugbear of British and American industry, the machinery which in Sweden is at once its guarantee and its expression is worthy of detailed study.

Sweden was not always so happily situated. Early industrialisation at the end of the nineteenth century and the sudden exploitation of Norrland brought with them much industrial distress. The labour movement was revolutionary, communist or anarchist. When, in 1931, workers demonstrating against blacklegs were fired on by troops at Ådalen, and several workers were killed, matters had reached a dangerous crisis. Only the Social Democrat victory at the polls in 1932 took it off the boil.

The upshot of Ådalen and the great depression was the Saltsjöbaden Conference of 1938. At this resort in the Stockholm Archipelago, management and labour sat down to establish a machinery which would give the country labour peace. Even today, when the going seems to be getting too rough or tough, the "Saltsjöbaden spirit" is often invoked. Today, labour and management face each other as two balanced, opposing, but not hostile forces.

All trade unions are affiliated to the Swedish Federation of Trades Unions (*Landsorganisationen*—LO). Its 41 one-union-per-industry unions comprise 1,550,000 workers, more than 90 per cent of the entire non-white-collar labour force. White-collar workers are represented by the Central Organisation of Salaried Employees (*Tjänstemännens Centralorganisation*—TCO) with half a million members, and about 45 per cent of all white-collar workers. A third, recently rather militant organisation, is the Confederation of Professional Associations (*Sveriges Akademikers Centralorganisation,* SACO), representing some 70,000 academically-qualified persons.

On the other side of the table, management is organised in 46 associations. All belong to the Swedish Employers' Federation (*Svenska Arbetsgivareföreningen*—SAF), whose 2,500 members employ altogether 1,200,000 persons.

Without any interference from the State, these top-level organisations try to arrive at overall wage-agreements for one-, two- or even three-year periods at a time. Both wield a good deal of power over their members, SAF particularly so. Every labour contract made by an individual employer must have

SAF's approval. The forty-one national trade unions, on the other hand, are sovereign bodies, free to approve contracts or call strikes. But they are under an obligation to keep LO informed of all important disputes or wage movements. A union starting a strike which involves more than three per cent of its members forfeits the right to financial assistance from LO during the conflict. LO assists at wage negotiations, and is represented in all more important ones. TCO affiliates usually conduct their own.

Into such negotiations and such contracts legislation only enters at four points. (1) It protects the right of association on either side. (2) It makes existing contracts enforceable, and (3), where they are disputed, compels adjudication over their interpretation or application. And (4), in cases where deadlock is reached, the law requires the intervention of a government-salaried mediator, and insists on a week's notice of all strikes or lockouts.

The word *strejk*—strike—appears quite often in Swedish newspaper headlines. But it rarely means what it says. What is in question is a threat or notice to strike—a very different thing. Further, unless two months' notice is given before a contract's expiry, it is deemed to remain legally in force.

The two- or three-yearly nation-wide wage negotiations at top level are crucial to the whole system. All necessary statistical information having been supplied by the Statistical Bureau— a body whose objectivity no one doubts—the negotiations usually begin with a general debate on economic matters. The actual negotiations then follow. Often they are arduous and long-drawn-out. If, as is not infrequent, they reach a deadlock, one or more of the eight full-time salaried State mediators is called in.

The mediator, however, cannot force an agreement. The most he can do is to put a time-limit on his own intervention, thus forcing the negotiating parties to press on, often working day and night, towards a solution. Such marathon negotiations are dramatic features of the Swedish industrial scene. They are covered in detail by the press, and are regarded as something of a national drama, affecting everyone. Only if mediation fails is direct action resorted to.

From 1945 to 1969 Sweden had only suffered from three major strikes: metals, 1945, 5 months, 11,311,112 lost man-hours; food products, 1953; and school teachers, 1967. Thanks to the top-level "frame agreements" (*ramavtal*), everyone knew where he stood. Once entered into, a contract was binding all down the line, from the national federations down to individual employers and on the shop floor. Nor could resignation from a union free anyone from his contractual obligations.

But 1969 saw a couple of wildcat strikes which may bode a change in mood, and even call for a revision of the system. One of the industries to go on a month-long wildcat strike was the state-owned Kiruna iron mines, where, it was claimed, the manual workers' conditions were far from good. The strike cost the company a million kronor a day. But though the system may need revising, basically it works, and has worked magnificently for decades.

The Labour Court

This Court is competent to settle, definitively and usually very quickly, all matters of interpretation. It consists of a board of seven persons. Two are appointed by SAF, two by LO, and three—of whom two are experienced judges—are representatives of the public. Where a dispute affects TCO or SACO, their representatives replace the LO men.

The court has an extraordinary record. The trade unions' initial antipathy has long ago been overcome. About ninety per cent of all cases have in fact been submitted from the labour side. It should be noted that the court does not arbitrate: it adjudicates. And there is no appeal. It also assesses fines and damages. Although the Labour Court has so far dealt with upwards of 4,000 cases, these do not represent even one per cent of all disputes. Most have been settled out of court.

Individual matters, unjust dismissal claims, etc., do not come before the Labour Court, but before the Labour Market Council, which also can award damages.

Labour-management committees

The mutual respect achieved by labour and management for each other's point of view is also reflected in labour-management committees, found in virtually all concerns. Management is under an obligation to make known its investment and marketing plans, with a certain discretionary right to withhold information which might jeopardise its position against competitors. Workers are encouraged to submit creative suggestions. One year, when 13,000 such suggestions were sent in, more than half were actually applied.

Further, both labour and management have set up schools in industrial relations and economic techniques. SAF runs three; one for management training, another for supervisory training, and a third for training time-and-motion study men. TCO runs two schools for its own members. The basic idea is that both sides shall have sufficient fundamental education in industrial and economic problems to be able to "talk the same language."

Perhaps such a system could only work in a country whose citizens possess a strongly corporate psychology and a high degree of education in social planning, and who, during a few decades, have seen their standard of living soar to heights against which the lives of their fathers and grandfathers seem positively primitive.

EXPORTS AND IMPORTS

One Swede in four is working for export. Total export income in 1968 amounted to Sw. cr. 25,500 million (£2,500 million, $5,100 million).

In recent years, none of Sweden's traditional exports—iron ore, lumber, pulp—have grown as fast as total exports. Even though, absolutely speaking, the demand for semi-finished goods has not fallen, value-added products are rapidly overtaking them. Most of the export trade goes to Europe (78 per cent), and of this over half goes to Scandinavia, which Swedish industry has more and more come to regard as one large home market.

Traditionally, Britain is Sweden's largest customer. Today, 1969, she is her second largest, and also her second largest supplier. Especially since EEC came into being—although she has applied for full membership Sweden, chiefly because of her political neutrality, which she insists on retaining, is not a member—more and more exports have been going to the EFTA countries, of which Sweden is one.

On the import side, West Germany is Sweden's chief supplier, notably of machinery and finished products. Other important imports from Germany are chemicals (a quarter of all chemical imports) and nearly two-fifths of engineering imports.

Sweden also has a lively trade with the United States (7 per cent of exports, 9 per cent of imports). Here the changing pattern of Swedish exports is particularly noticeable. In 1953 more than three-fifths of exports to the USA were primary commodities— notably pulp—and only 5 per cent were engineering products. Today the latter dominate with 50 per cent and the former have shrunk to a mere 15 per cent. Half Sweden's imports from the USA are now engineering products and other finished goods. Food, fuels and raw materials make up another quarter. Japan and Canada are two other increasingly important trade partners, Japan being particularly close to Sweden nowadays, thanks to the SAS polar route.

Sweden also trades with eastern Europe, notably the USSR (4-5 per cent), exporting chiefly finished goods and engineering products and importing raw materials and fuels, particularly coal from Poland.

Though Sweden is whole-heartedly in favour of free trade, recent tendencies to set up trade barriers and common markets of the EEC type, and the high prices of Swedish goods, have obliged the Swedes to invest extensively abroad. Since 1960, such overseas investments have risen by 60 per cent, and today Swedish subsidiaries in other lands employ 156,000 foreign nationals. In 1965, some 450 Swedish firms had foreign subsidiaries, twice as many as five years before. Understandably, in view of the EEC barrier, West Germany is by far the most important region for such developments. In North America, on the other hand, where there have been no such trade barriers, Swedish investments have declined.

Foreign firms do not find it quite so easy to set up subsidiaries in Sweden. Although attracted to the flourishing market and the Swede's unexcelled purchasing power, such activities are seriously restricted by Swedish law, which limits the rights of foreign nationals or companies to acquire land, mines or shares in certain corporations, and makes all such acquisition subject to government approval. The exceptions in this respect are metals and chemicals, notably petrols, where the American oil companies predominate.

Nevertheless, the foreign business sector is growing faster than native Swedish enterprise as a whole. Such foreign manufactures as cars (German, Italian, French, American, British), electronics, business machines, plastics and photographic equipment compete vigorously with each other and with Swedish products. This gives the Swedish shopper a freer choice and consequently a sharper and more demanding sense of quality than perhaps any other European today.

At present the foreign share of total manufacturing in Sweden is still no more than five per cent. In no single industry is the foreign share more than one-fifth.

INDUSTRIES

Forest-Based Industries

Sweden's conifer forests seem to the eye to be infinite. Actually they cover about 55 per cent of the land surface of the country. It takes the best part of a century for a stately pine (40 per cent) or spruce (44 per cent) to grow to full stature, particularly in Norrland, where the climate is more severe; yet every year the increment is an estimated 56 million cubic metres. At present one-third of a man-day is necessary to process every cubic metre of felled timber, and in the near future it is hoped to reduce this time to one-tenth of a man-day. In 1968, 110,000 workers were engaged in felling and hauling timber in the forests, a force which, thanks to automation and mechanisation —log-floating on the great Norrland rivers is steadily yielding to motor haulage—will probably have fallen to about 90,000 by 1970. At the same time the output value for the forest-based industries, Sw. cr. 38 thousand million (£3 thousand million, $7.6 billion) in 1950, had risen to Sw. cr. 122 thousand million (£9 thousand million, $24 billion) by 1966. A quarter of these vast forests is owned by the State, another quarter by private companies, and the rest by farmers. The larger corporations dominate the north.

The largest part of the timber crop goes to the sawmills for lumber-processing and for chemical pulp, groundwood or fibre building-board. From the era of felled lumber, in the mid-nineteenth century, the industry moved into the chemical pulp age, which in turn has been giving way to paper and board production and other by-products.

At the same time, the relative importance of the forest industries, compared with other sectors, has declined. Their share of Swedish exports before World War II was 40-50 per cent: By 1967 it had dropped to 27 per cent. Most of the output is exported to western Europe, chiefly Britain and the EFTA countries.

The sawmill industry processes 40 per cent of the annual cuttings. In 1966 its production exceeded 2.1 million standards. In volume, lumber exports have risen by 40 per cent since the war, but their share in value of total exports has fallen from 11 to 6 per cent in the same period. Britain, which used to be a leading customer, now buys only 25 per cent of the total, the rest going mostly to western Europe.

Wood-based panel products, plywood, blockboard, fibre board and particle board are all of growing importance. The 700,000 tons of fibre building board produced in 1967 represented about 12 per cent of world output, Sweden, with her 400,000 exported tons, coming second only to the USA in this field, with about

40 per cent of the world total exports. The home market, too, has a higher per capita consumption than any other country.

From 1950 to 1967 the pulp industry, Sweden's former great staple, more than doubled its output: 5.4 million tons of chemical pulp in 1967, and 1.3 million tons of groundwood. More than half the total volume is market pulp, of which 90 per cent is exported, the concentration being on bleached pulp and kraft. Nearly 10 per cent of the world's chemical pulp comes from Sweden.

In 1967 paper manufacture, mostly for packaging, amounted to Sw. cr. 3.3 million (£264,000, $660,000) and the output is rising by 8 per cent per annum. The packaging industry is on the way to outstripping the world's newspapers as the chief customer. The Swedes themselves rank only second to the USA as per capita consumers of paper (320 lb per year). With two million tons going abroad in 1967, Sweden is one of the world's three leading exporters of paper and board, 42 per cent of her exports going to Britain and West Germany. As a paper-manufacturing nation Sweden takes ninth place.

Swedish matches, which once were so dominant on the world market, are now only a minor industry relatively speaking. They

---

The SAAB Mach 2 fighter "Draken" (J 35 F) currently in service with the Royal Swedish Air Force.

The ASEA company of Vasterås specialises in large high-tension electrical equipment.

come from the Swedish Match Company's plant at Jönköping, in south-central Sweden, and are made, not from pine or spruce, but aspen wood, of which Sweden, also has plentiful quantities.

Mines

Although Sweden's forests are more striking to the eye, her mining and metal-working and engineering industries, with Sw. cr. 38,816 million (£3.15 thousand million, $7.76 billion) of the GNP, head all statistical tables for output and productivity. Between 1949 and 1966 Swedish mines nearly doubled their output, with an almost unchanged labour force.

Iron ore has long been a most important Swedish staple, and her resources are still estimated to be at least another 3,700 million tons of ore; unlike most of the world's ore seams, the Swedish seams become broader the deeper they lie. Of the 28 million tons produced in 1966, 85 per cent came from the three greatest mines, of which two—the Great Iron Mountain at Kiruna and Malmberget ("The Ore Mountain") in Northern Lapland—lie seventy miles north of the Arctic Circle. The third large mine, Grängesberg, lies in central Sweden. About 95 per cent of the output was exported, Sweden's exports of ore, measured in

-----

The Royal Palace at Stockholm in winter. The sailing vessel *Af Chapman* (foreground) is a youth hostel.

The Stockholm satellite of Farsta; it is centrally heated by nuclear energy.

G

shipment value, being the third largest in the world.

To climb up to the top of the Ore Mountain—the heart of which has been gouged out like a vast bath with terraced sides— in the light of the midnight sun is a most unusual experience. The iron content of this ore (60-70 per cent as compared with 38 per cent of the French or 32 per cent of the German ore) is the world's richest. But it is also relatively rich in phosphorus, which has to be corrected by dressing. It is then shipped by the world's northernmost railway, the electric ore line, which climbs over the Norwegian mountains at Riksgränsen and descends to the ice-free port of Narvik.

The oldest Swedish iron-mining region is Bergslagen, into which Walloon miners immigrated in the seventeenth century. Although many of these ancient mines are now no more than picturesque relics, a considerable number of small mines in Västmanland, Västergötland, Värmland and Dalarna provinces are still operating profitably. All are dominated by one large producer, the Grängesberg Company.

Sweden's share of world iron-ore output has fallen from a mid-nineteenth century 40 per cent to a mere 3 per cent. But 25 million tons are mined annually, and make up 6 per cent of all Swedish exports, and a sixth of the world's.

Of non-ferrous metals, the largest deposits are in the north. Although quite a few mines are State-owned, the Boliden Company does all the mining. There are a variety of ores: copper, zinc, lead, pyrites, gold and silver. Laisvall is Europe's largest lead mine.

Iron and steel

Sweden is famous for her high-grade steels, indispensable for everything from the barrels of guns to razor blades. Though based on her ore deposits in the far north, most steel works are not in Norrland, but in Central Sweden. All, except the Luleå works in Lapland, which produces about 10 per cent of the annual output, are owned and operated by private enterprise.

A higher proportion of Sweden's steel output than any other country's goes to high-grade steels, and accounts for three-quarters of total export value (1.36 million tons: Sw. cr. 2,070 million, £160 million, $415 million). Total output of finished steel in 1968 was 3.63 million tons, and of crude steel 5.1 million tons.

Swedish stainless steel is also famous. The two most important steel towns are Eskilstuna, between Örebro and Stockholm, and Sandviken, near the Baltic port of Gävle. They bear scant resemblance to an old-style industrial city, and are as bright and polished as their own products.

Engineering

This is the largest manufacturing sector, employing about 400,000 people, or nearly forty per cent of the total labour force. Of these, nearly one in three is a white-collar worker—a figure indicative of the crucial role played by research.

Starting in the sixteenth and seventeenth centuries as nail factories—the nail forges founded by Rademacher are still a tourist sight at Eskilstuna—Sweden's engineering industry now specialises in such high-grade and sophisticated products as ball and roller bearings, a Swedish invention (SKF or "Skefko"), sewing machines (Huskvarna), weapons (Bofors), electrical machinery, giant turbines and long distance high-tension cables (ASEA at Västeras), tungsten-carbide drills (Sandviken and Fagersta), and drilling equipment (Atlas Copco) vital to the iron-mining industry, milk separators, another Swedish invention (Alfa Laval), automatic lighthouse beacons (AGA), office machinery (FACIT), and cars (Volvo, SAAB, Scania Vabis).

A very important engineering sector is the electrical. The L. M. Ericsson Co is one of the world's most important firms in telecommunications, and has been enormously successful in obtaining contracts for whole countries' telephone and telex systems—for example, Australia, Brazil, Mexico. Another firm whose name has a familiar ring, both in Britain and America, but which is Swedish-owned, is Electrolux AB. Precision, which might be said to be a built-in trait of the Swedish character, is a vital element in all Swedish engineering. The micro-gauge was invented by a Swede, C. E. Johansson, a valued colleague of Henry Ford I.

Of engineering exports, 40 per cent go to EFTA countries (Sw. cr. 26 thousand million, £2 thousand million, $5.2 billion in 1966) and 20 per cent to EEC. On the import side, Swedish engineering products have a stiff fight with foreign competitors. From her Scandinavian neighbours Sweden imported them to a value of Sw. cr. 820 million (£65.6 million, $164 million), in 1966, and also heavily from West Germany, a traditional source. About one-third of all Sweden's engineering needs are met by imports.

Shipbuilding

In 1965 and 1967, Sweden ranked second among the world's shipbuilding nations. She produces between 8 and 10 per cent of the world's annual shipping output. Her chief customer is her seafaring neighbour Norway. In terms of tonnage, big tankers and bulk carriers constitute about 87 per cent of this output; but a higher value per ton is represented by smaller cargo vessels, refrigerated ships etc.

In shipbuilding the high Swedish wage-levels have made themselves sharply felt, and therefore automation and rationalisation have come to play a vital role. Just how vital one can see by standing in, for instance, the Arendal yard at Gothenburg, where large vessels are built indoors and slowly pushed out section by section on to the slips. A mere half-dozen men, sitting at control panels, seem to be in charge of this complex, high-precision operation.

The State has not helped the shipbuilding industry in any way, unless guaranteeing its credits may be considered a type of subsidy. Swedish shipyards, therefore, have to compete on unequal terms with countries like Japan, whose shipyards are heavily State-subsidised.

The yards are concentrated on the west coast, at Uddevalla

and Gothenburg, and in the south at Malmö (Kockums AB). The latter company is preparing to build tankers in the half-million-ton class.

Electric power

Derived from the great rivers of the north, a plentiful supply of hydro-electric power has been a crucial factor in Sweden's arrival as an industrial country. Water is the chief source of energy (93 per cent). On the other hand, Sweden has so far no liquid fuels or natural gas at all, and half of her domestic consumption comes from imported oil, only 8 per cent from coal, also imported. Since power consumption is rising by about 5 per cent per annum, and electricity generation by 6-7 per cent the country is also in a position to export electricity to her Scandinavian neighbours, notably Denmark. Only Norway, Switzerland and New Zealand are as reliant on electricity as Sweden, with her 5,350 kilowatt-hours per capita of population.

In 1965, 45 per cent of all electricity was generated by hydro-electric plants belonging to the State Power Board, 39 per cent from sources belonging to private enterprise, 13 per cent by local authorities, and 3 per cent by other producers. All the electricity is retailed over a national grid, and much comes south over the 3,300 miles of 200,000-volt DC lines invented and manufactured by the ASEA company. (The Franco-British line under the English Channel uses the same system.) Though the supply of water varies greatly between summer and winter, the abundance of lakes makes regulation an easy matter. The largest hydro-electric power stations are deep underground, hundreds of feet beneath the bedrock. About 60 per cent of output is utilised by industry.

In the province of Västergötland, Sweden has significant deposits (about a million tons) of uranium, from which about 120 tons of pure uranium are being extracted yearly. The first atomic energy station was opened in 1963 at Agesta, outside Stockholm. A second is being developed at Marviken, in Östergötland, and a third near Oskarshamn, on the south-east Baltic coast. In 1965 a uranium mill at Ranstad, in south-west Sweden, with a capacity of 120 tons a year, started operation. In 1966, for the first time, more nuclear thermal than hydro-electric stations were opened.

Other industries

Two other important industries are cement and concrete, where two firms account for 90 per cent of all output, and glass, including, of course, the famous Swedish ornamental and domestic glass. The latter is mostly made in rural but highly modern and sophisticated factories in Småland.

There is also an important textile industry. Centred at Borås, near Gothenburg, it had a difficult period in the 1950s and early 1960s, with many closures and mergers. But it has fought back against international competition, by automation and capital-intensive methods, until today it is said to have a higher overall technical level than any of its foreign competitors. Mechanical plant in the spinning and weaving mills is valued at Sw. cr. 130,000 (£10,000, $25,000) per production worker, a good deal more than the national average. Imports supply the Swedish market with 50 per cent of textiles and 20 per cent of all wearing apparel; there has recently been a notable rise in textile imports from EFTA countries. Exports, on the other hand, are based wholly on superior quality and design—a designer in Sweden earns perhaps four times what his British or American colleague can count on. From a mere Sw. cr. 140 million (£11.2 million, $28 million) in 1959, sales in foreign countries have soared to Sw. cr. 725 million, (£58 million, $145 million) in 1967.

Tanning, too, is a very old Swedish industry. Today the tanneries produce light leather for shoe uppers and wearing apparel. Rising costs have proved almost insuperable to the shoe industry, and many of its small factories have closed or merged. In the rubber industry, including the manufacture of car tyres by Trelleborgs Gummifabrik AB, synthetics now play a very important part. A Swedish invention which has been widely adopted is the inflatable building, made of synthetics : even in the depths of the Swedish winter it can be used on building sites and to house materials, or indeed for almost any other purpose for which temporary shelter is needed. Sweden's main export market for rubber products is the other Scandinavian countries.

Chemicals and chemical products, notably oil and petrol, have been much affected by the inflow of American capital, which has set up joint enterprises with Swedish firms. The sixties have seen the establishment of a petro-chemical industry and a rise in chemical output of about 10 per cent a year. One of the largest firms is Mo Domsjö AB, at Örnsköldsvik, on the coast of the Gulf of Bothnia. In 1966, Sweden manufactured 600,000 tons of sulphuric acid and 227,000 tons of chlorine—nearly 2 per cent of world output. Mostly it is manufactured in connection with pulp mills.

The most important feedstock for organic synthesis is ethylene, a hydrocarbon. At Stenungsund, in Bohuslän, the Swedish Esso Company has erected a steam cracker with a capacity of a quarter of a million tons of ethylene a year, most of it being used for the plastic polyethylene. Mo & Domsjö process ethyl alcohol, a by-product of sulphite lye and agricultural alcohol, to make such things as butanol and octanol.

Production of plastics has risen by about 20 per cent a year since the war, and in 1966 passed the 200,000-ton mark, of which about a quarter went to export. The biggest single export item here is decorative plastic laminates for kitchens.

Lastly, Sweden is the land where dynamite originated—a vital product in a land with a granite bedrock. Invented by Alfred Nobel, it gave him the fortune from which he founded the Nobel Prizes.

The Motor Industry

There are two car firms : Volvo, in Gothenburg, and SAAB (The Swedish Aeroplane Co) in Linköping. A third firm, Scania Vabis, manufactures lorries and buses.

From being a purely indigenous car, built and designed for rigorous Swedish winter conditions, the Volvo has become a prime export article. Volvo AB is, in fact, the largest single export firm in the country, with a turnover of Sw. cr. 1,400 million (£120 million, $280 million), or 5 per cent of the entire national export figure. The Volvo works, outside Gothenburg, employs 26,000 workers and is expanding to use a further 6,000. A Volvo bought in Sweden is automatically guaranteed for five years—a guarantee which passes on to anyone purchasing it second-hand. Production of cars in 1968 reached a figure of 170,000 passenger vehicles and 12,400 commercial vehicles. More than one-third of car exports go to the USA, where Volvo is one of the most popular European models.

The SAAB, a smaller car, has like the Volvo repeatedly taken home the laurels in many an international rally.

Agriculture

Notwithstanding her high degree of industrialisation, Sweden is agriculturally self-supporting. No doubt she would not be if the same severely competitive principles were applied to her farming as to her other industries. But considerations of defence, and also the political alliance which used to exist between the Social-Democrats and the former Farmers' Party, have led to extensive subsidisation of agriculture.

Such subsidies, however, have not been applied in a haphazard way. The State considers that out of a total area of 6.4 million acres of arable land, at least a million would do better if turned into forest; a characteristic of Swedish farming is that sixty per cent of all Swedish farmers also do forest work. As the flight from the land continues, and an ever-higher degree of mechanisation becomes vital, small farms become less and less viable, and fiscal and other measures are forcing mergers into larger units. The average farm size, 12.8 acres, is thus steadily growing, as has happened in other highly developed countries. Today the active agricultural population is only 215,000 people, or 6.3 per cent of the active population as a whole. Over 90 per cent of all agricultural land is privately owned, and less than 20 per cent is used for human foodstuffs, 40 per cent for hay, and over 35 per cent for barley, oats and mixed grain. Between 800,000 and 1.2 million tons of wheat, and the same amount of oats and barley, are harvested each year. The potato crop is about 1.6 million tons, and the sugar beet crop about 1.5 million tons.

It is chiefly southern and central Sweden, with their great plains, which offer really profitable farming land. In spite of the northerly latitude, intensive treatment of the soil has raised its yield to usual European levels. The most notable farming district of all is Skåne, in the far south, where the Findus canneries have their great farms. Down there, under the wide Skanian sky, farming has become a highly technical and experimental industry, producing such notable things as "chromosome pigs," twice as large as the ordinary porker. As one travels into Norrland, on the other hand, the countryside seems ever more depopulated, both of men and beasts. Often one comes across *ödegårdar*—abandoned farms—where the life work of generations of hardy peasants, wresting a meagre living from the encroaching forest, is being allowed to return to the realm of nature. In striking contrast to the modernity of the cities, the old wooden farmhouses and the great barns have mainly the old people to attend to them—people without the ability or the desire to adapt to the new urbanised Sweden.

5

How They Learn

SWEDEN was not the first Scandinavian country to provide universal schooling for her citizens; Denmark was. But the Swedish system dates from 1842, and it has always set its stamp on the nation's affairs; also to some extent, no doubt, on the national character. Based originally on Prussian models, for all generations up to the latest there has been something distinctively disciplinarian about going to school. All Swedes of the older generation have gone through this mill, vividly satirised and attacked in Ingmar Bergman's famous film *Frenzy* (1945). Perhaps its chief products have been a passion for facts and figures, and a curious deference to expert authority —even in matters where it may not be really warranted. Exams, indeed, have been something of a Swedish nightmare. The *studentexamen*, which used to give the right to wear the coveted white-topped "student cap," was abolished in 1968, being regarded by the Social Democrats as undemocratic—that is, unegalitarian. But the fact remains, the more egalitarian a society becomes, the more competitive it must be : and the greater the hegemony of the exam.

The new school system, however, with its firm and universal basis in a nine-year comprehensive school (*grundskola*), aims at undoing many of the mistakes of the past, and lays much greater stress on personality development. No longer will Swedes toil over long hours of homework and go anxiously to school merely to be cross-examined on the results—breeding in the Swedish psyche a strange view of life, perhaps, as one big exam. Many educators, however, maintain that the new system, in doing away with old vices, is also threatening to put an end to old virtues, and that it is lowering standards crucial to Sweden as a modern industrial society.

Today, 17.7 per cent of the national operating budget, Sw. cr. 5,500 million, (£440 million, $1,100 million) goes to education and research. Of this, 64 per cent comes from the State and 36 per cent from the regional authorities. All but the largest municipalities spend at least half their budgets on education. It is this sort of investment which Swedes are referring to when they speak of the Sweden of the seventies as "the educational society," and of an "educational explosion."

All but a tiny minority of Swedish children—mostly diplomats' children and children of other Swedes living overseas—attend the co-educational national day schools. The academic year, forty weeks long, lasts roughly from the latter part of August to 10 June, with two holiday weeks at Christmas, one at Easter and a winter sports vacation at the end of February, when thousands of schoolchildren cram the winter sports hotels along the Norwegian border. School begins at 8.30 am, and goes on until 3 or 4 pm. After each 40-minute period all children— whatever the weather—go out for a ten-minute breather. Swedish schools are without exception very modern, many strikingly so. Their very appearance is testimony to the size of public investment in this sector.

Oddly, Swedish children are generally not mature enough to start school until the age of seven. The fact is, they are late starters—modified American IQ tests valid for children aged five are applied to Swedish children two years later. Before seven, some 250,000 children attend either kindergarten or nursery schools; but Swedes generally regard the British habit of sending tiny children off to school at the age of four or five as queer and cruel. On the other hand, the first year at a Swedish school is definitely above the kindergarten level.

COMPREHENSIVE SCHOOLS

At seven, all Swedes start comprehensive school. This is a nine-year school, divided into three 3-year sections. That is to say, compulsory schooling ends at about sixteen years of age, and is followed by a voluntary two- or three-year theoretical or trade school for pupils aged seventeen to twenty, to prepare them for the university or jobs in society. All instruction, from the first day to the last, is free, and there are also free lunches, free school equipment, free books, and free medical attention.

The junior level of the comprehensive school, comprising grades 1-3, is taught by a one-class teacher. Except for a few obvious subjects, like music and physical training, there are no streams or specially-taught subjects. Almost all teachers in junior schools are women. They earn about Sw. cr. 2,500 (£200, $500) a month. The one-class teacher system is also retained in middle school (grades 4-6), half the teachers being women on an average monthly salary of Sw. cr. 2,900, (£232, $580).

Compulsory subjects in lower and middle school are Swedish, mathematics, religion, provincial culture (which graduates to civics, history and geography in middle school), music, handicrafts and gymnastics. English, Sweden's second language, is taken from the fourth grade on, and is regarded by all as very important, if only because so many films and TV programmes are in English. And it is in fact surprising what good English quite small Swedish children will speak; often much better than their parents or grandparents. A recent study reveals that, after seven years of English, the average Swedish child has an active vocabulary of 690 words, and a passive one of 1,900. The only two words universally understood by all pupils were "bed" and "crocodile," which is easily understandable, seeing the words are virtually the same in Swedish. Language teaching has gone over to modern language laboratory methods, with a strong emphasis on speaking and understanding spoken English. The British accent is *de rigueur*.

As to the teaching of religion, there has been a great deal of opposition to it, and its opponents, who are vociferous in the newspapers and the Riksdag, point out that to indoctrinate children with Christianity is incompatible with the United Nations clause about freedom of religion. So far, however, nothing has been done about taking religion out of the school curriculum, though parents can easily get their children exempted if they file a special application.

At the seventh grade and the beginning of senior school, subject teachers are introduced, and a choice is given between certain optional courses in languages (German or French), art, economy and technology. English may now be dropped, but in fact some 90 per cent of all pupils elect to go on with it. In 1966/67 a second foreign language was a favoured choice with 82 per cent of all pupils. Not until the last year of comprehensive school, however, is there any streaming.

SECONDARY EDUCATION

Entry from comprehensive school into secondary school, whether grammar school (*gymnasium*), continuation school (*fackskolan*) or vocational school (*yrkesskola*) is based on the pupil's marks in grades 7-9 of comprehensive school. Formerly there were three sorts of gymnasium—technical, commercial and general. These have now been merged. The new gymnasium, superimposed on the comprehensive school, gives three years of education in five curricula: humanities, social sciences, business-economics, natural sciences and technical arts. There is also a core of common subjects, supplemented by a number of subjects specified to each of the five curricula. Pupils who graduate with a specific grade average are entitled to enter one of the country's five universities or a professional school. Thus there is no longer any eqivalent of the British O- or A-level exams. But by the time he or she leaves the gymnasium a Swedish child has a smattering of three languages, as well as the beginnings of a specialised education fitting him or her for higher instruction in that line. About 30 per cent of all pupils attend the gymnasium.

An alternative to the gymnasium is the continuation school. A two-year supplement in the fields of social sciences, economics and technology, it gives mostly theoretical preparation for practical occupations, and about a quarter of each age-group goes this way. Completion of its course, however, does not qualify a student for university.

A third line of secondary education is the vocational school. According to present estimates (1968), 35 per cent of the country's seventeen-year-olds will be attending vocational school in 1970. That is to say, 85 per cent, of all Swedes of that age will be receiving secondary education of one sort or another.

To encourage such engagement of young people in educating themselves, special study grants are payable. At present a monthly allowance of Sw. cr. 75 (£6, $15) is paid to all secondary school pupils, providing they have begun their studies before the age of twenty-one. Subject to a means test, there is a further grant of Sw. cr. 250 (£20, $47) per month. For those who start secondary education after the age of twenty-one there is a somewhat smaller allowance.

UNIVERSITIES

There are five universities. The oldest, founded in the sixteenth century, is at Uppsala, followed in order of seniority by Lund, in Skåne, Stockholm, Gothenburg and, recently added, the university at Umeå in Lapland. In certain other towns (Örebro, Växjö, Karlstad, Linköping) there are newly-established affiliated universities, qualified to grant first degrees in the humanities and social and natural sciences.

It is at university level, of course, that the current "educational explosion" is most marked. In 1945 there were only about 14,300 undergraduates. By 1955 this figure had increased to around 22,600, by 1964 to over 58,000, and a figure of 87,000 is predicted for the early seventies. Pressure is particularly great on the science side; a number of lines have had to be blocked—accepting only the most brilliant aspirants. This is one reason why, at present, the humanities are attracting nearly four times as many students as the natural sciences (42,350 as against 11,420), resulting in a dangerous imbalance. Theology, law, medicine, technology, dentistry, economics, pharmacy and miscellaneous subjects absorb the rest. It is estimated that the number of persons holding academic degrees will double itself every thirteen years.

Such degrees are prefixed to the name of the holder (*Fil. kand., Fil. lic.*) and should not be omitted when writing him or her a letter. For teachers there is an intermediate grade, *Fil. mag. (Filosofie magister)*, between the *Filosofie kandidat* and the *Filosofie licentiat*. To the *Fil. lic.* degree a doctor's thesis is usually all that is wanting to secure the most coveted title of all—*Doktor*. Though not so common in Sweden as, for instance, in Germany, it is not exclusively used when addressing doctors of medicine.

Recently there has been much heated discussion about the structure of higher education. In the spring of 1968 a report by a government commission, UKAS, precipitated an explosion of wrath among students. Hypnotically impressed, perhaps, by the action of the—quite differently situated—Sorbonne students, the Stockholm students "did a Sorbonne" and "occupied" their club house. No doubt some of this was mere histrionics; but the fact remains that a vital principle was at stake. UKAS wanted to tighten the choice of subjects and in various ways integrate university studies yet more closely with the machinery of Swedish industry and administration. In this respect the Swedish tradition differs sharply from the British; there is no industrial or commercial scorn for what is academic. The principle of disinterested liberal education, the radical students felt, was in serious danger; they saw themselves doomed to ever deeper enslavement in the economic establishment. And they did not lack supporters in the press and among the public. The matter is still under review, but the UKAS plans have already been modified by government.

Swedish students, however, can hardly compare their situation with that of their Parisian colleagues—or if they do, then it reveals a marked lack of a sense of humour. Compared with the Frenchman, a Swedish undergraduate enjoys, generally speaking, exceptionally good conditions. Great numbers, if by no means all, live in specially-built blocks of one-room student flats (converted into tourist hotels in the summer months), and all qualify for interest-free loans of up to Sw. cr. 8,000 (£640, $1,600) a year. Admittedly, such loans have to be repaid afterwards. But there is also a small monthly cash allowance (£140, $350 a year). An undergraduate with one child to support can claim a total amount of Sw. cr. 9,400 (£752, $1,880) a year.

At neither Uppsala nor Lund are there any equivalents to England's Oxford or Cambridge colleges. Instead, the old medieval tradition derived from the Sorbonne of "nations," clubs rather than colleges, has survived. All students from any one province belong to the same "nation." Altogether, student life at Uppsala is much less collegiate and social than it is at Oxford or Yale. Students seem to live much on their own in their flats or lodgings, come and go as they like, and study fairly intensively. The old happy days of the upper-class student

———————

Dancing round the midsummer maypole.

Christmas, the festival of the home in the dark Scandinavian winter. The four Advent candles are lit successively for each Sunday in Advent.

who, never passing his exams, spent his life in a happy dream of intellectual indolence, romantic male-voice choir singing, and alcoholic indulgence, have gone. Instead, the student corps (*studentkåren*) is a centre of intense political discussions; studies are closely correlated with advancement in the social and industrial grades in later life; and the pressure of expectations too often proves too heavy.

ADULT EDUCATION

Another aspect of the educational explosion which has deep roots in the Swedish past, and in Swedish habits of mind generally, is adult education. Every autumn, as the evenings swiftly draw in, some one million adult Swedes—one-eighth of the entire population—turn out in the cold to flock to adult classes. By far the most popular and numerous are language classes; notably, of course, classes in English. Organised by a wide variety of bodies, local libraries, the ABF (Workers' Educational Association) etc, the classes all receive State subsidies in proportion to the numbers of their pupils. Swedes are great people for qualifying themselves and keeping up with the times; and the

---

Typical central Swedish landscape.

"Flying Angels", one of the groups of sculpture by the late Carl Milles to be seen at "Millesgården", outside Stockholm.

H

educational explosion, giving all children nine to eleven years schooling, threatens to leave the adults behind.

Adult education can be more or less haphazard, or directed and purposeful. At present, Sweden is re-schooling a higher percentage of her adult population than any other country. Vocational training at fifty centres throughout the country is providing for 70,000 adults. About 2,000 more are enrolled at two State adult and secondary schools.

People's High Schools

Another 12,000 are studying at 105 State-supported People's High Schools, the *Folkhögskolor*. These were also a Danish invention, but they have played an important part in the development of modern Sweden. All are residential colleges out in the country, and all have their roots in some popular movement, often religious, co-operative, temperance or political. But although the aims of the parent movements may be at odds, the aims and goals of the *folkhögskolor* are strikingly similar: to provide higher and essentially liberal education for adults who, for economic or other reasons, have missed it in their teens. The average age of students is quite low: twenty for girls, and twenty-one for boys. A large percentage have held jobs before coming to the college. Their backgrounds are usually extremely varied.

Of the People's High Schools, fifty-seven offer three-year and forty-six offer two-year courses. There is wide freedom of choice in subjects—in fact, one might almost say that only in these adult education colleges is there the typical campus atmosphere of an American college, or the liberal love of study for its own sake that used to characterise British universities, the free and wide-ranging discussion. Swedish university studies totally lack the tutorial dimension—sometimes the professors seem so far above the heads of their students that the latter make little contact with them. But at a *folkhögskola* students and teachers live together and join in all sorts of communal activities (somewhat less so today, perhaps, since the advent of the car has made it so much easier to go home at week-ends). Some of Sweden's most distinguished citizens, authors and public figures who have come from working-class backgrounds have educated themselves in such a college. Foreign students can also attend the *folkhögskolor*, of course, and there has been a considerable amount of interchange, particularly with the USA.

6

How They Get About

In the past Sweden, with its widely scattered population, was a country of few roads and bad ones. Travel was easier in winter than in summer, a horse-drawn sleigh moving comfortably along the tracks in the forests and even more speedily across the endless miles of frozen and snow-laden lakes. Before the railways arrived in the 1850s, and for half a century thereafter, most summer travel, at least in south and central Sweden, was also by water. Nowadays the little black-and-white lake steamers, with their tall funnels, their saloons where elderly gentlemen sat drinking their *punsch*, with their heaps of baggage piled on the foredeck, are but a nostalgic memory. A few steamers still ply between the more important communication points and islands in the Stockholm Archipelago, a mere one or two still make occasional excursion trips on the Mälaren Lakes, while elsewhere some ancient steamer is kept in service by a local tourist association. The historic Götal Canal, between Gothenburg and the east coast, is still used, by eighty-year-old steamers in the summertime and by the occasional Baltic timber schooner. But the lovely trip across the huge lakes of central Sweden and through the ninety old canal locks designed by Telford, the Scottish road-builder, is mostly patronised by foreign tourists. Otherwise, steamers have been completely ousted by the car.

In Sweden, the railway age and the steamer age coincided; each was a facet of the country's nineteenth-century opening up to travel and commerce. Today the railways are waging a courageous but losing battle, not only against Europe's highest per capita car density, but also against rapidly expanding domestic air travel. From carrying two-thirds of all passenger traffic in the 1950s, the railways are now carrying less than a fifth. On the freight side the railways' prospects do not look so bleak—in 1968 more freight was carried by rail than by road.

As for sleighs, they are occasionally brought out at Christmas-time for a trip to church. Their modern descendant is the caterpillar-track "snow weasel," which scuttles about in the frozen wastes of Lapland, bringing provisions and other goods. Here and there, on a country road, one may still come across some older person on a *sparkstöting*—a chair on steel runners, propelled vigorously by a driver who, standing on one runner, kicks rhythmically with his other foot as he and his passenger fly along over the snow. Over the fields and fells and through the forest tracks a pair of skies, propelled by ski-sticks and long-legged strides, is still as good—and certainly as healthy—a mode of transportation as any.

ROADS

Like all other aspects of industrialism, the motor age arrived late. Anyone visiting Sweden after World War II was more likely to be struck by the great numbers of bicycle-stands to be found everywhere in the streets, attached to the front of buses, and on railway platforms. Today, the pushbike has almost vanished, giving way in the fifties to the motorbike and the moped—the international term originated in Sweden—and in the sixties to the car.

From having had almost no tarmac roads in the forties, Sweden today has some extremely fine ones. Of the GNP, some two per cent is being spent on road-building. As has been said, the ratio of cars to population is more than one to four, making Sweden the most highly motorised country in Europe. By the beginning of the seventies the figure is expected to reach the current US level. Once again, one is struck by the enormous swiftness of the transformation.

Today there are 68,000 miles of roads. In south and central Sweden all trunk roads are tarmac, but, as one travels into Norrland, fewer and fewer are. There are 200 miles of linked motorways—a figure which by 1985 will rise to 931 miles. By-roads are everywhere mostly gravel.

The word "density" in connection with cars, or indeed with anything else in Sweden, is, however, misleading. With so small a population and so large a country, even when there is one car to every three inhabitants, which will happen soon, driving in Sweden will remain a far more spacious experience than in the rest of Europe. In the far north it can be quite an event to meet another car.

In the cities, of course, the picture is different. As early as the late twenties the Stockholm authorities began work on the famous "Slussen" cloverleaf traffic-way, which, poised over the old water sluice on the south side of the old town, and with an underground railway bridge passing through the entire complex, absorbs traffic from seven directions, spins it round and spews it out again. Even more elaborate systems have recently been constructed. To the west of the city the new Essingeleden's high, graceful bridges span a limb of the Mälaren lake.

In all city centres parking is severely restricted, notably in Stockholm, Gothenburg and Malmö. But in Stockholm there are five great underground garages, intended, as has been seen, for nuclear shelters in wartime. One lies deep beneath the new Hötorget shopping centre. Parking rates are very high at 1 kr an hour.

A most impressive piece of social engineering where the Swede's apparently innate capacity for corporate action really came to the fore, was the changeover to right-hand driving on 3 September 1967. Not only did every single traffic sign—and Sweden seems to have more than her share of traffic signs—all traffic lights and lanes etc have to be switched : it had to be done overnight. In this potentially murderous operation every man, woman and child was mobilised, having been informed by mass media many months in advance. Schoolchildren and the aged had to be particularly firmly re-schooled. On the crucial day all traffic stopped for six hours—in the cities for twenty-four. When, after a delightfully traffic-free Sunday, it started moving again, it crawled along at speeds the Swedes hadn't seen since the motor car was first invented. Gradually the speed limits were eased, and traffic flowed again—with a *lower* accident rate than before. No highly-publicised event could have been better calculated to show Sweden at her organisational best.

One advantage following from the changeover is that Swedish motorists can now see where they are going. Traditionally, they have always imported cars from right-hand drive countries; and as long as they drove on the left, overtaking was a nightmare.

Of the 213,103 cars sold in Sweden in 1968, 26 per cent were Volvos and 15 per cent SAABs. Other favourite makes are Volkswagen, Ford (both British and German), Mercedes, Opel, and Plymouth.

RAILWAYS

Virtually every stretch of railroad track in Sweden is owned and operated by the Swedish State Railways (*Statens Järnvägar, SJ*). Although many branch lines have been shut in recent years in the name of economy, the rail network still amounts to about 8,000 miles of track, equal to the distance between the North Pole and South Africa. In proportion to population it is the largest mileage in Europe: 11.8 miles per 10,000 inhabitants. On the other hand, most is single-track, and trains have to wait for each other to pass through stations. Only some of the main lines in the south and central regions are double-track. The battle against road and air transport has led to a keen rationalisation, especially in the use of labour.

There are three types of passenger train: (1) the *express*, usually a low-slung articulated train set of three or four cars, travelling almost non-stop at speeds up to 82 mph, and covering the distance of 340 miles between Gothenburg and Stockholm in 4 hours 10 minutes, (2) the *snälltag*, an express train which only stops at major centres and, unlike the *express*, is composed of normal carriages; and (3) the *lokaltåg*, or stopping train—nowadays usually composed of railcars.

Ninety per cent of all passenger rail traffic is electrified, the rest being diesel. The track is European gauge, but the carriages are somewhat wider than usual. This makes for spaciousness and comfort. Almost all the passenger rolling-stock has been replaced during the 1960s, and the new second class is so comfortable that SJ is said to be finding it difficult to sell first-class tickets. In every *snälltåg* will be found special compartments for mothers with small children (*barnkupéer*). These have their own miniature toilets, and sleeping racks for the toddlers and babies. There are also special compartments (*hundkupéer*) for passengers travelling with dogs. In the Pullman coaches and compartments the windows are double-glazed, many carriages are air-conditioned, all are centrally heated, and the general impression one has when stepping on board a Swedish train is that it has just come from the factory—and a very clean factory at that!

Sleepers have three bunks in the second class, and two in the first. If you want a sleeper compartment all to yourself, then you have to pay a double first-class ticket. Sleeper ticket prices do not vary (Sw. cr. 19 in 2nd, 29 in 1st), irrespective of length of journey. With some 3,200 persons sleeping in its *wagon-lits* every night of the year, SJ boasts of being Sweden's largest hotel.

The SJ policy is gradually to abolish all local rail traffic, reserving the line for fast medium-distance trains that can compete with the car and with air services. On the other hand, SJ also operates the largest network of bus services in the country, which links up with the trains.

The cost of rail travel falls sharply the longer the journey. A second-class journey for 310 miles costs Sw. cr. 82 (£7, $16.40) while one of 620 miles costs only Sw. cr. 115 (£9 10s, $23). Children go for half-price between the ages of six and twelve, and for a quarter-fare where two other persons are travelling on full fare, or even if one of them is another child at half-price. There are also round-tour tickets for tourists.

The Scandinavian Airlines System is a world-wide network with a high international reputation. Three-sevenths of its shares are owned by the Swedish Government, the other four-sevenths equally by Denmark and Norway. The other two countries sometimes complain that Sweden preponderates unduly in the company's affairs; but in reality SAS seems to be scrupulous in its tri-national responsibilities. SAS is perhaps the most effective single instance of practical Scandinavian co-operation. In 1968 SAS had a total revenue of $293.5 million (£121 million) of which $16.6 million was profit, and carried 4.2 million passengers.

SAS over-the-pole flights to Tokyo in 1960 made aviation history, and the regular route then established is now a part of world geography. The SAS route via Tashkent is also a pioneer achievement. DC8s, Coronados, and Super-Caravelles are currently flown on the short-haul routes in Europe; daily connections are made between Kastrup airport (Copenhagen) and most European capitals, and with New York and the Far East.

Sweden's domestic air services, like those of the other two countries, are operated either by SAS directly or by AB Linjeflyg, a subsidiary.

Small aircraft are much used for getting about in the northern regions. Taxi flights can be taken from such places as Porjus and Kiruna, and the Lapps themselves frequently use helicopters to get up to their mountain pastures; small Sea-Bee seaplanes are a usual mode of transport between one lake and another. Even fishing tours of this sort are offered to the tourist. In a country as advanced as Sweden, private aviation is likely to become much more common, the thousands of lakes offering potential airfields in winter if skis were fitted.

THE ÖRESUND BRIDGE

Sweden is separated from Denmark and the European land-mass by the narrow Öresund Strait. For many years plans have been in hand to span it with a great road and rail bridge, which would have profound economic and perhaps also psychological importance. Discussion has run high as to whether the bridge should run from Elsinore (Denmark) to Hälsingborg (Sweden)— the narrowest part of the straits or between the two great cities of Copenhagen and Malmö. A feat of bridge-building which is already far advanced is the 2,191 ft Öland Bridge, at Kalmar. When opened for traffic in 1972 it will be Europe's longest bridge. Its chief function, however, will be touristic. Öland has no large towns or industries.

The Merchant Marine

Most of the ships flying the blue-and-yellow Swedish flag today are fast motor vessels, plying either to the Far East or Australia or the west coast of the United States. Of 1,062 vessels, 146 are tankers, aggregating 435,000 gross tons. There is also a sizeable fleet of coasters and short-sea traders plying the coasts of western Europe and the Mediterranean.

The three crowns of Sweden on the funnels of the great white passenger vessels of the Swedish American Line are a familiar sight in the Hudson River, in summer bringing American tourists to Europe and Scandinavia, and in winter cruising the Caribbean. The line is part of the Broström concern, which is said to be the world's largest group of companies. The little black-and-white Baltic timber schooners which used to be so numerous around the coasts and in the great lakes of central Sweden have almost disappeared.

FOREIGN TRAVEL

Out of eight million Swedes, well over a million go abroad every year on holiday. Somewhat naturally, their first choice is Mediterranean sunshine. But in 1968 more than 100,000 visited Britain, one of their main reasons for doing so undoubtedly being to "polish up their English." For the distance involved, travel across the North Sea by the car ferries of Swedish Lloyd (Tilbury-Gothenburg), Tor Line (Immingham-Gothenburg), and Ellermans Wilson Line (Hull-Gothenburg), is exceptionally cheap. Other Swedish tourists went to France (180,000), Italy (330,000) Spain (334,00) and Germany. Some 27,700 Swedes visited the USA during the same year, mostly, of course, on business.

Incoming tourism cannot balance such a massive outflow of travel expenditure. Tourist receipts amount to Sw. cr. 811 million (£65 million, $162 million). Notwithstanding the fact that 178,228 Americans and Canadians, 151,670 Englishmen and 550,000 Germans, to name only the most important categories, visited the country in 1968, there is a big and steadily increasing tourist deficit. Sweden, at least in summer, has a lot to offer tourists, at least those who still know how to enjoy those dwindling luxuries, space, natural beauty and fresh air. But for all its long hours of sunshine, her summer is short, she has no real Alpine downhill skiing in winter, and she is a high-cost country. Realisation of this, and also a traditional deprecatory attitude towards their own country's charms, have limited the Swede's belief in their own capacity to attract tourists. "So have we a deficit in the balance of payments in oranges—but no one's suggesting we grow oranges!" commented the big daily newspaper, *Dagens Nyheter* on a proposal that the tourist industry needed more investment. Compared with more southerly countries, or even with Denmark and Norway, Sweden treats tourism as something of a Cinderella among industries.

7

Swedish Thinking

THE Swedes make a great deal of what they term their "public debate"—a debate carried on in newspapers and other mass media. In a foreigner's eyes, however, "debate" seems the wrong term. It is usually, indeed, very lopsided. Intellectual life is to an extraordinary degree a prey to fashion, even more so than in Britain and the United States.

That received opinion should be generally radical is doubtless in part a result of the swiftness of sociological and economic change; the changes which, within a mere half-century, have precipitated Sweden from being a backward agricultural society into being an ultra-modern and industrialised one. On the other hand, one can see the radicalism as a cause of such thorough-going change. In letters to the editors of the more conservative-minded newspapers, disgruntled individuals express their irritation and bewilderment at the rate at which everything is going and the outrageous libertinism of dominant ideas and policies. But no coherent conservative philosophy can really be said to exist.

Nor is radicalism just a matter of opposition. Sweden must be one of the few countries on earth, if not the only one, to have a government which, after thirty years in power, is still radical-minded. One reason for this is the characteristic Swedish habit, or if one prefers, trick, of co-opting into the régime any independent critic who may arise, and by making him a member of an *utredning* (commission), putting him in a position to rectify such abuses. In this way change is combined with stability, and radicalism does not generate tensions of a sort which in other countries would lead either to revolution or violent reaction. What, then, are the radicals so radical about?

HUMAN PROBLEMS

To say that Sweden is the first country in history to have solved her citizens' economic problems, levelling out the spread of wealth without loss of civil liberty, is, of course, an exaggeration but it contains a truth. And where material problems are no longer acute, hitherto latent spiritual problems will come to the fore. To the older generation of Social Democrats it has perhaps been something of a surprise that, even after three decades of enlightened rule, the old Marxist theory that all spiritual problems are really nothing but material ones in disguise still remains unproven.

The public debate since the war has therefore been less preoccupied with material than with strictly human problems; notably with questions of value. Where, for instance, in a secularised society, can a basis be found for morality and ethics? What are the sanctions and guide-lines of the good life?

The thinking and also the actions of the last two generations of Swedes have been dominated by the Uppsala philosophy, whose founder was Axel Hägerström (1868-1939); a philosophy known as *värdenihilism*—"nihilism of values." According to this way of seeing things, value judgments ("this is right, that is wrong, this is good, that bad") lack descriptive philosophical status; that is, they are meaningless as descriptions of reality. Such categories, to the value-nihilist, are mere personal exclamation marks and real life becomes a very technical affair, devoid of emotional overtones. Obviously a highly Swedish philosophy, *värdenihilism* has been deeply responsible for the dispassionate way in which the the undeniably practical Swedes have sorted out their affairs. It has also been in practice the philosophy of the Social Democratic régime, in whose eyes the function of government is simply to provide all material conditions for culture, but in no way to dictate what that culture's spiritual content shall be. The State is neutral. It is an efficient machine.

Sweden can be seen as a striking and advanced instance of the movement, visible in all western societies, away from the "status" society; away, that is, away from the old medieval scheme in which an individual's destiny was in a manner fixed from the outset by his or her status, towards an open society where he or she is free to make decisions and can only be bound by free contract. The older sort of society assumes a right to dictate moral attitudes, to decide what a citizen may or may not read, or see, what he should think, say or do. The new does not; it is inherently foreign to all ideas of censorship.

THE SEXUAL REVOLUTION

In the immediate post-war period Sweden gained the reputation of being a land of free love. Foreign journalists, visiting Sweden to find food for thought or for their readers' indignation, have been apt to take Swedish statements on sexual matters at face value. It is also true that in their urban and industrialised society the Swedes have retained a basic peasant tradition in sexual matters. The strict moral conventions of the nineteenth and early twentieth centuries which temporarily overlaid it have been roughly thrust aside, and are today generally regarded as merely hypocritical. In theory! But not, it seems, in practice! In 1968 a large-scale Swedish "Kinsey" Report, more thorough-going than its American prototype, mapped out present-day Swedish sexual attitudes and habits.

To everyone's consternation—not least, of course, the foreign journalists' and TV producers'—it was found that in the previous twelve months 90 per cent of all married Swedes had been faithful to their spouses. Either 1967-68 had been a sabbatical year or there was something definitely wrong with the prevalent picture of Sweden as the land of promiscuity and free love.

Yet, though 87 per cent of all Swedish men and 91 per cent of all Swedish women regard "fidelity within marriage as absolutely necessary," and by their behaviour show that they live up to their belief, the report shows that attitudes to premarital intercourse are liberal. Even among those who attend the services of the State Lutheran church, 71 per cent of all men and 64 per cent of all women regard intercourse permissible to a couple who are in love (among nonconformists 44 per cent and 42 per cent respectively); and 90 per cent of all who attend the State church (80 per cent of nonconformists) regard it as permissible between affianced couples.

The condition of such an acceptance of pre-marital sex relations is an insistence on birth-control. The study reveals that two very definite moral canons have come to prevail among present-day Swedes, replacing the taboos of a society which knew neither birth control nor social responsibility for illegitimate children. First, where a child is not definitely wanted it is regarded as immoral *not* to use contraceptives. Second : "Two persons should not start a sexual relationship if either knows it will disturb an already existing one with someone else." As to the former rule, about one-third of all those interviewed admitted they did not always live up to it.

In such a climate censorship will obviously no longer play any significant role, and during the last ten years it has in fact been virtually swept away. The crudest pornographic publications are found in tobacconists', newsagents' and bookshops. Except for children under fourteen, there is no longer any film censorship. In 1968 Europe's first public exhibition of pornographic and erotic art opened in the southern university town of Lund. Old-age pensioners, brought in bus-loads, found the pictures "intriguing." Neither they nor anyone else—except the usual few writers of letters to editors—had any objections, or wished to expose themselves to the charge of old-fashioned "Anglo-Saxon" prudery.

The sexual revolution has been swift. Its successive stages are marked by such facts as that, while in 1938 it was still against the law to spread information about birth control, by 1946 it had become obligatory for all chemists to sell contraceptives; in 1958 sex education was made obligatory in all schools.

The sexual revolution, however, should not be seen in isolation. It is part and parcel of the great radical wave which is still sweeping Sweden and Scandinavia generally. It is not merely age-old Christian values, or more recent Victorian values and prejudices, which are being questioned. Everything is.

THE WOMAN QUESTION

This much-debated issue is not to be confused with the sex question. Many observers have noted a latent tension between the sexes in Sweden. Swedish men are apt to refer to women as *fruntimmer* and women talk equally scornfully of *"karlar"*— two untranslatable terms which, on the lips of the opposite sex, imply the inferiority and general moral turpitude of those to whom they apply. Something of this archaic relation between the sexes perhaps lies behind what is portentously called the *könsrolls-fördelningsfrågan*—the question-of-the-respective-life-roles-of-the-sexes. The issue is one of the most hotly debated in recent years. The Swedish woman, so famed abroad for her independent status and spontaneous attitudes, declares herself—or by her protagonists is declared—to be in fact a downtrodden slave, and compares her status with that of the negro in the deep south of the USA. By this she does not mean she has not got the vote; she won it in 1919. Nor that she is not legally her husband's equal: the law explicitly declares her to be so, and where no special contract of marriage is drawn up to cover the matter, she is legally entitled to half the joint property in the event of divorce. The law also declares that she, as much as her husband, is legally responsible for the support of their children.

The quarrel is therefore not primarily one of legal status. Nor is it merely personal. Like everything else in Sweden, it is rational and socio-economic.

A housewife may or may not be a slave. What is more serious—it is pointed out—is that she is a slave who, in the era of washing machines and deep-freezers, is no longer even needed. A Swedish economist calculates that Sweden's already high standard of living could be raised by a further 50 per cent if all married women who are not mothers of very small children went out to earn their own livings. At present some 46 per cent do—in Stockholm. Elsewhere, notably in Norrland, there is a high level of female unemployment; immeasurable, in fact, since so many married women who would like to go out to work do not even apply for jobs which, in Northern Sweden, are scarce.

Further, scientific studies have revealed that the children of working mothers are no worse adapted to life than the children of stay-at-home housewives. "It is the quality, not the quantity, of the parent-child relationship that counts."

The cry, therefore, is not merely for more nursery schools, but for a society in which men and women will be really and truly equal. Where, for instance, half the cabinet would automatically consist of women; where every other prime minister would be a woman; likewise half the directors of all companies and of all the higher ranks of the civil service; where "men should look after their babies as much as women do" and therefore have a legal right to a periodic leave of absence from their jobs to attend to their families. Above all, a society where in all branches of industry, women would earn the same wages for the same work as men and in which suburbia, with its lonely, half-employed housewives, would be swept away.

Only a few writers of angry letters to the editor plaintively ask where the arts of home life would be if there were no housewives? And whether everything must be sacrificed to the material standard of living?

Yet the *könsrollsfördelningsfrågan* is no mere piece of feminine melodrama, either. It is based on the insight that the old agrarian society, which flourished in Sweden up to fifty years ago, has passed irremediably away; and with it the co-operative homestead family, where father, mother, grandparents and children all worked together creatively. Instead, Sweden, like other western societies, now has the "transitional family," where father goes out to work—and very often has to overwork—while the meaner burdens of existence are still the "prerogative" of

I

the housewife—even though she may be as highly qualified as her husband to do more interesting and useful work. It is high time, say the protagonists in the woman question, for the life-roles of the sexes in modern society to be analysed in the light of modern conditions. Society's "status" allocation of roles to men and women must be radically revised.

THE NEW CONSCIENCE

If the immediate post-war generation was deeply struck on sex, and Swedish films have made their triumphal progress through the world's art cinemas largely because of it, that generation's children, now grown up, have made a *volte face*. Suddenly, they are interested in quite different matters. And their attitudes are bewildering to their seniors.

Among younger Swedes the only respectable attitude today is to be not merely enlightened, but *vänstervriden*—"twisted to the (new) left." Their shibboleth, as in all other western countries, is the Vietnam war.

For centuries the Swedes have lived a peripheral existence. Since the Thirty Years War, in the seventeenth century, history has left Sweden largely on one side. Up to very recently, emotional and ideological isolation, a certain smugness, detachment, an objective better-than-thou attitude, has been the hallmark of their neutrality.

But now the younger generation is turning savagely on all such neutral "value-nihilistic" smugness.

"How can we Swedes dare to pretend we are neutral or morally superior," they say, "when two of our largest companies are building a road in Thailand, from which US bombers are attacking North Vietnam? It is sheer hypocrisy! And so is all talk of Sweden being a socialist country. Or even an enlightened one. As long as our economy is a by-product of the western economy at large, Sweden is just as deep-dyed in the white man's imperialism as the USA, Britain or Russia."

Value-nihilism explodes in a violent bellyache of conscience—

the old Swedish puritan conscience no doubt, in secular guise. No other country's newspapers are currently devoting anything like so much space as the Swedish press to the dilemmas and troubles of the poor "Third World" and the exploited countries of Asia and Africa and South America. Swedish writers like Jan Myrdal, Sarah Lidman, and Per Wästberg go to China, Afghanistan or Angola, and come back with personal reports of the miseries endured by the black, brown and yellow races, still the victims of the white man's economic, if not political exploitation. They see the world through the eyes of the oppressed. And a whole younger generation of Swedes seethes with indignation.

This moral *volte face* is not confined to a preoccupation with Vietnam and Angola and Greece, either. More Swedes live alone—as has already been pointed out in this book—than in any other nation on earth. And, indeed, emotional and social isolation has been the paradoxical aspect of Sweden's so well-integrated society. The roots of this chronic *ensamhet*—this loneliness—are complex. The younger generation sees it as an emotional deep-freeze; the nemesis of a life without moral commitment. The emphasis is therefore now on *gemenskap*—a new "togetherness." Traditionally, a Swedish Christmas is the festival of home and family; for those who do not belong to such a group, psychiatrists comment that a Swedish Christmas can be a terrible experience, bringing numbers to psychiatric clinics in a state of nervous breakdown. But at Christmastime 1968 the young people of several major cities, inviting the lonely, the old people, the drunks and outsiders to one long Christmas party, celebrated an entirely new sort of Christmas; a Christmas more in accord with the spirit both of socialism and Christianity. There is to be an end to *ensamhet* : to loneliness, that bane of the new urban milieu. And an end, also, to non-commitment.

8

How They Amuse Themselves

THE *dolce far niente* of Italian life, the French *bistro*, the pleasant nonsense talked in English pub or American coffee house, are all equally remote from the style of Swedish living. Lack of any such informal and unconstrained gathering-places is, indeed, one of the admitted shortcomings in Sweden's social pattern. In a northern land, where snow lies on the ground for more than half the year and outdoor temperatures can stand at around −20°C for weeks on end, the necessary dialectic between work and play has to take other forms. Above all, it becomes a seasonal affair. Caught between their high standard of living and their icy winter, the Swedes sensibly devote the winter months to work and the summer to leisure.

But winter, too, has its breaks, notably at Christmas. Christmas is a long-drawn-out affair lasting from 13 December when St Lucia, the patron saint of light (brought to west Sweden by Irish missionaries in the ninth century) takes on the comely form of a Swedish blonde with a crown of lighted candles on her head, and appears early in the morning, bearing coffee and buns to the paterfamilias, to Twelfth Night, which is a public holiday. Swedes cheerfully remind themselves that Christmas, in Sweden, is of pre-Christian origin. Viking habits of immoderate eating and drinking, like the Christmas ham—which in their esteem is what turkey is in Britain or America—are relics of old midwinter sacrifices.

Easter, too, a three-day holiday, marking the approach— if not yet the arrival—of spring, is a welcome relief in the daily round. Swedish housewives welcome it with gaily coloured chickens' feathers, tied to sprigs of silver birch: the "spring" sunshine, gleaming on the snow outside the window, together with the central heating in the sitting-room, bring out the green leaves before any other greenery except, perhaps, a lonely snowdrop, has yet appeared in nature.

Midsummer is celebrated not at the solstice itself, but at the nearest week-end—usually the third in June. By then the nights have shrunk to nothing, and a silver twilight of two or three hours—in the north nothing at all—separates one day from another. Midsummer Eve is the day when the maypole— an old Viking fertility symbol—goes up in every farm and town and village, and in country districts, notably Dalarna, people put on folk costume to dance around it. All this may read like a tourist brochure. But Sweden's agrarian society has only so recently been displaced that its old seasonal festivals are still very much alive, lending a considerable charm to the annual round.

The seasonal contrast also goes far to explain the pull which *Naturen*—nature, the great outdoors—exerts on the industrialised Swede. A holiday for him, is essentially a getting-away-from-it-all. At summer week-ends the flight from the cities seems almost manic, and a summer week-end in Stockholm, particularly in July, can be quiet indeed. Everyone is away.

As has been said before, the *sommarstuga*—summer house— is an important part of a Swede's life. With the great increase in leisure time, the State is encouraging all sorts of outdoor activities, and subsidising holiday villages where summer houses can be rented by the week. Some have recently become popular with visitors from abroad.

Attached to a summer house, more often than not, is a boat. It used to be said that more Stockholmers owned a boat than a car; this is probably no longer true, but the return of the small-boat fleet to the capital on a summer Sunday evening is an impressive sight. In all the town's many creeks and waterways are boat and yacht clubs. In the archipelago, right on his door-step, the Stockholmer can sail for weeks on end, literally without ever having to navigate the same stretch of water twice.

With all these natural advantages, one wonders why so many Swedes go abroad in the summer. In winter it is more understandable. The Swede is exchanging his traditional pleasure—a bracing "walk on skis"—for the beaches of the Costa Brava and Majorca. Not that winter sports do not flourish. Ski-jumping and slalom are both widely practised, and hardly a community with a hill in the vicinity does not exploit it for a ski-jump, with illuminated trails all round. Other Swedish winter sports are ice-hockey, curling, tobogganing, and "bandy" —a game of eleven-a-side ice-hockey, played on a rink the size of a football field.

The "Vasa Race," the biggest ski race in the world, is run on 13 March each year. It commemorates a turning-point in the fortunes of the country in the early sixteenth century, when skiers from Mora—where the race ends—set off towards the Norwegian border to fetch back Gustavus Vasa from his intended exile. By no means all the 5,000 entrants complete the arduous course.

Football (soccer) is played in summer and is extremely popular. But there is no professional football, all teams are amateur. The State-run football pools organisation (*Tipstjänst*) arranges for Swedes to bet on British league games, so that the names of many British cities are as familiar in Sweden as they are in Britain.

A Swedish sport which has begun to catch on in other countries is "orienteering." The contestants, equipped with compass and maps, are taken to some remote spot in the forest or countryside, and have to find their way home again. Mammoth relay races, in which hundreds of people of all ages take part, are often run on these lines. It calls for good physical condition and a flair for map-reading, often at night.

TV AND RADIO

All broadcasting is the monopoly of the Swedish Broadcasting

Corporation (*Sveriges Radio/TV*). This independent company, financed by licence money, has much the same status and constitution as the British Broadcasting Corporation. Although commercial interests have agitated incessantly for American-style radio and television, this has been "definitely rejected" by the government after close consideration of the evils which have followed from independent commercial TV in Britain, and, even more, in the USA. A notable reason given for adhering to a State-monopoly has been the restricted programme choice which paradoxically ensues from fierce listener competition. The opening of the second non-commercial TV channel (TV 2) in 1969 is widely regarded as having clinched this matter for good, though the international TV satellite system many nevertheless one day force it to be modified.

At the same time the Swedish Broadcasting Corporation is being organised to give maximum independence to its various services. Thus TV 1 and TV 2 each has its own separate organisation. Regional autonomy is secured to some extent by giving the regional offices complete freedom to produce whatever programmes they wish with their budgets. Since such programmes cannot be broadcast regionally, as the country as yet cannot afford separate regional TV channels, they are offered to TV 1 or TV 2, whose programme directors are free to accept or reject them. Special stress is laid on educational broadcasting: both in TV and radio it comes under an entirely independent division of the Corporation.

At present there are about three million radio licence holders and over two million TV licences. This is a density (29.5 per cent) approximately the same as in Britain, and represents the fastest rate of expansion of any European country.

NEWSPAPERS

The Swedes have a voracious appetite for newspapers. For every 100 persons, 53 papers are sold every day, a figure which puts the Swedes at the head of the world newspaper-reading league (USA 32, Britain 48, France 24). Two or three Stockholm newspapers (*Dagens Nyheter*, circulation 434,512, *Svenska Dagbladet*, 151,700, and the evening papers *Expressen*, 455,900, and *Aftonbladet*, 272,200) have a nationwide readership and therefore can be regarded as national papers. But certain papers published in the provinces have comparable status: notably *Göteborgs Handels och Sjöfarts tidning*, *Göteborgs Posten* both published, of course, in Gothenburg, and *Sydsvenska Dagbladet*, published in Malmö.

Despite a strong tendency for the weaker papers, through small circulations, to go to the wall, the large newspaper chain or syndicated column is unknown and the provincial press has a strongly independent profile of its own. Political and editorial debate is by no means confined to the national press. This good tradition is stimulated by the major papers' pleasant habit of quoting other newspapers' more striking opinions in a special column every day.

Since the population does not seem to be large enough to support more than a very few specialised intellectual magazines (but *BLM—Bonniers Litterära Magasin* is said to have a bigger circulation than any other literary journal in the world) the duty of discussing ideas, however abstruse, falls entirely on the cultural columns of the daily press. On the other hand, there is no equivalent to the British Sunday newspaper: the daily papers, come out seven days a week.

Both the largest papers, *Dagens Nyheter* and *Expressen*, are owned by the Bonnier family, who also own the country's largest book-publishing house and, through Åhlén and Åkerlund, publish 50 per cent of all weekly magazines. Culturally radical, the Bonnier family are politically liberal, but their papers are not tied to the policies of any one party. *Göteborgs Posten,* liberal, with the third largest circulation is owned by its editor; and *Sydsvenska Dagbladet* is also a family-owned paper. Doyen of the press, but strongly conservative, is *Svenska Dagbladet*, which, since 1940, has been vested in an independent foundation, whose board consists of "representatives of private enterprise, cultural institutions, public and private administration and defence, together with the editor and managing director."

It will be seen that the circulation of the press does not reflect the party allegiances of its readers. Commanding over half the electoral body, the Social Democrats have never been very successful with their own newspapers. *Aftonbladet* is the only major socialist paper, though there are a number of smaller ones.

For this reason, no doubt, but also to stem the tide of newspaper deaths, the Social Democrat government, in the autumn of 1968, passed what was originally designed as a press subsidy law. Subsidies, taken out of a public 25-million kronor fund, will be paid out to the political parties in proportion to the number of seats held by them in the Riksdag. The measure was strongly resisted by liberals and conservatives, whose newspapers have never needed any such subsidies. And in reality the parties are not obliged to use these funds to subsidise only newspapers.

Freedom of the press is guaranteed by a paragraph in the constitution, which may only be altered after dissolution and re-election of the Riksdag. It is a freedom under responsibility. Each paper must have an *ansvarig utgivare* (responsible publisher), who may or may not be the actual editor. It is he who, if he publishes defamatory material, can be sued. A similar law limits liability in film production. On the other hand, both the responsible editor and his staff are protected by a noteworthy law which guarantees any journalist against being forced by the authorities, or indeed by anyone else, to disclose the source of published information. In fact he is forbidden to do so, and nor do the police have any privilege in this respect. Thus the "little man" can feel safe in bringing what he considers an abuse to the notice of the press.

On the other hand, the press may not abuse its privileged position. *Pressens Opinionsnämnd*, a body similar to the British Press Council and set up jointly by the Association of Swedish Newspaper Proprietors and the National Press Club, issues judgments on whether, in any case brought to its notice, a journalist or newspaper has "offended against good newspaper practice." This verdict the offending newspaper is then required to publish in its own columns, and copies are sent to all other papers.

Perhaps the prime job of the press, in Swedish eyes, is to reflect discussion of public issues and keep a sharp eye on the powers-that-be. No one who has ever held an official position in Sweden and has had anything to do with the press will have failed to notice how conscious newspapermen are of this duty. In a country where the bureaucrat has so much to say about everything, this is just as well.

BOOKS AND WRITERS

Sweden has only a few authors of the first rank, the most famous of them being August Strindberg (1849-1912). But she has a substantial literature, both traditional and modern. Her present output of books is remarkable : about 7,000 volumes a year, as compared with 29,000 for Britain and 59,000 for USA, with a population twenty times as great. Admittedly 1,452 were translations, and of these 974 were from English. In the world league in book production Sweden stands in fourth place.

Swedish authors lament the limitation imposed on them by writing in a "minor" language. There are many grants and scholarships, but few writers can live entirely on their literary work. A form of aid to writers which seems only just is the 6 öre (about 1d, or 1c) a Swedish writer gets each time one of his books is borrowed from the public library.

The Author's Association is at present pressing for this sum to be raised to 25 öre. The public library system's per capita book stock is about 2.5. Book-buses and book-boats circulate in the countryside and archipelagos.

The Swedish Academy, founded 200 years ago by Gustaf III, has eighteen chairs, and to occupy one of these is the ambition of even the most radical writers. The Academy also awards the annual Nobel Prize for Literature, the largest of all literary prizes. Most of the recipients have been too famous and aged to be much in need of the Nobel Foundation's generous cheque, and the Academy can hardly be said to have heeded Alfred Nobel's wish that "the prize shall go to that writer who *during the last year* has produced the most distinguished work of literature of an idealistic nature." On the other hand, the international character of the prize has drawn attention to writers in languages far away from Sweden and Europe.

The Social Democrats have recently introduced a system of life-grants to Swedish writers, artists and composers. At present 150 such "cultural workers," whereof 20 are authors, are being guaranteed an annual income of at least Sw. cr. 30,000 (£2,400, $6,000). Any earnings are deducted from the grant. Both the method and the persons selected have come in for criticism, but the system is regarded as a first step towards giving writers something of the same sort of security as is enjoyed by other Swedish citizens. It is also in line with Social Democratic welfare philosophy; the individual should not be crippled by economic anxiety. On the other hand, his desire for the "cream" of existence and its luxuries can be depended on to stimulate his output.

LITERATURE

Swedish literature hardly began before the eighteenth century. It contains little or nothing from the Renaissance, and very little—apart from the visionary works of Saint Bridget—from the Middle Ages. Early poets wrote drinking songs, or modelled themselves on the French writers of the seventeenth and early eighteenth centuries. The first independent Swedish genius was the great song-writer Carl Michael Bellman (1740-95), whose remarkable *Fredman's Epistles* and *Fredman's Songs* are without their like elsewhere in literature. In drastic pen-strokes Bellman evokes the low life of eighteenth-century Stockholm. He was also a lyricist of the first order and his works are remarkable in being conceived to music, popular airs of the eighteenth century to which they are still sung. The song lyric as an art form is still much alive in Sweden today, and Bellman's songs are perennially popular.

Afterwards, still led by the poets, came romanticism, a vein which survived in Sweden later than in the rest of Europe, even up to World War II. But it is a romanticism which covers a wide gamut, from the early nineteenth-century poets E. J. Stagnelius (1793-1823) and P. D. Atterbom (1790-1855), the epically-minded Esaias Tegnér (1782-1846), the late nineteenth-century novelist and Nobel prize-winner Selma Lagerlöf (1858-1940)—her most internationally famous novel is *The Story of Gösta Berling*—and E. A. Karlfeldt (1864-1931), at one end, to the pungent, lyrical realism of Gustaf Fröding (1860-1911) at the other. Nor should the novelist, poet and dramatist C. J. L. Almquist (1793-1866), one of the most idiosyncratic of Swedish geniuses, be overlooked. In the mid-nineteenth century August Blanche (1811-1868) wrote vivid short stories of Stockholm life, fully comparable to the best European writers of that time, which as a picture of a bygone yet fully recognisable Sweden are still delightful to read.

But the genius who overshadows all Swedish literature—Bellman alone excepted—is August Strindberg (1849-1912). A brilliant prose-writer and poet, and the first realistic historical playwright of modern times, Strindberg in the 1870s was one of the angriest of all young men. A paranoid personality and a social critic of the first order, Strindberg, in his own phrase, was "tearing down to let in light and air" to a decidedly decadent society. His novels *The Red Room* and *The People of Hemsö* are classics. *Miss Julie* is possibly the greatest one-act play ever written in any language. Much obsessed by "the woman question" and an enemy in this respect of the Norwegian Ibsen, who used to refer to him as "the madman," Strindberg was a searing analyst of modern marriage (*The Father, The Dance of Death*, etc). Strindberg's realistic period came to an end with a phase of semi-insanity in Paris, his so-called "inferno crisis." Partly as a result of his experiences at that time, he created the modern symbolist drama, of which he is the consummate master, (*A Dream Play, To Damascus* and *The Ghost Sonata*). Almost all Strindberg's important works are now available in excellent translations.

The same peaceful revolution in Swedish society which grew from the labour movement and the rise of social democracy led, in the nineteen-twenties and thirties, to the emergency of the so-called proletarian writers. Most popular of these is Vilhelm Moberg (b. 1898), whose *The Emigrants* trilogy is the vividly-living memorial of the great emigration to America.

World War II and its anxious aftermath brought to birth the so-called *fyrtiotal*—the writers of the forties. Deeply influenced by T. S. Elliot, Kafka, Pound and Joyce, but also by the French existentialists—Ingmar Bergman's films are in the last resort more existentialist than anything else—the poets of the forties, led by Eric Lindegren (1910-1968) and Karl Wennberg (b. 1910), wrote many-dimensioned, modernistic poetry of an obscurity which, even allowing for the high status which poetry enjoys in Sweden, the public at large can hardly be said to have absorbed. A somewhat romantic and lyrical reaction set in in the fifties.

Today's writers are going abroad for their themes, and to a high degree identifying themselves with the developing countries and with the exploited peoples of the world. They are in revolt against their own tidy, smug society, and its *värdenihilist* attitudes. This calm, cool way of seeing things finds fine artistic expression in the novels of P. O. Sundman, whose *The Expedition* has recently been translated into English. In some ways Sundman's vision gives the most authentic account of everyday life in Sweden, at least as it has been since the war.

PAINTING AND SCULPTURE

Sweden is in a way one big art gallery. Great numbers of modernistic statues and other works of art are to be seen in all public places, both outdoors and indoors. From the spectacular Stockholm Town Hall (1911) onwards, public buildings have

been lavishly adorned with works by the most prominent contemporary Swedish artists.

Sweden has never given the world a Rembrandt or Cézanne.
But the Swedes have always had a great tradition of applied
art. Though their style may have accorded no more with the
tastes of western Europe than did their behaviour, the Vikings
were magnificent goldsmiths. Their heavy gold ornaments, still
to be seen in Swedish museums, are masterly. The coming
of Christianity at the end of the eleventh century and the
influence of a decadent romanesque style put an end to this great
native flowering of decorative art.

Toward the end of the Middle Ages there arose in the Stockholm district (Svealand) an indigenous, if German-influenced,
school of church painters. At that time the old parish churches
out in the countryside were being vaulted over and their flat
wooden ceilings, which had been brilliantly painted, were being
taken down and replaced by plastered brick vaulting. At the
expense of various patrons, many of these churches were now
entirely repainted, the medieval world of legend and Biblical
story entirely covering their walls and vaultings. The most
vivid and human of these painters was the Stockholm jeweller
Albertus Pictor (d. 1509), who at the end of the fourteenth
century painted the interiors of many fine churches, notably
those at Härkeberga (just off the Stockholm-Oslo road, near
Enköping), at Bromma and at Täby, both the latter now being
in the suburbs of Stockholm. Another great painter, with quite
another but no less beautiful, if less realistic style, was Johannes
Rosenröd, who in 1437 painted the church at Tensta, in Uppland. There are also many lovely painted churches in Skåne
and the south. Later centuries broke out large windows in these
originally small dark churches, especially in the north walls,
which had been great frescoes, and spoiled them. But the vault
paintings have survived, and many of the wall paintings have
been rescued from their whitewash. Sweden has some 500
painted churches, more than any other country in Europe. Yet
they are little known, even to Swedes.

Another famous work of late medieval art is Bernt Notke's

(d. 1496) "St George and the Dragon"—complete with maiden— in Stockholm cathedral. This painted sculpture group com- memorates the victory of the Swedes over the Danes at the battle of Brunkeberg in 1471.

The Isle of Gotland, too, has preserved a remarkable amount of fine limestone sculpture from the Gothic era. Uniquely in Sweden, it has also preserved some of its churches' lovely medieval stained glass.

It was not until the eighteenth century that Sweden could again be said to have produced any notable painters, and then of a wholly European and international type. The miniaturist Per Adolf Hall (1739-93), the court painter Carl Gustaf Pilo (1711-1793), and the portraitist Alexander Roslin (1718-93), could all equally well be French rococo painters—indeed Roslin worked in France. On the other hand, the *genre* painter Per Hilleström (1733-1816), and Elias Martin and his brother Johan Fredrik Martin, are much more Swedish, at least in their subjects. Elias Martin's delightful watercolours of the Stockholm of those days, also celebrated in Bellman's songs, are unsurpassed for their delicacy and freshness.

Without any question Sweden's greatest sculptor was Johan Tobias Sergel (1740-1814). His statue of the actor-king Gustaf III stands on the quayside just below the royal palace.

Nineteenth-century romanticism is perhaps best represented by Marcus Larson (1825-64), some of whose waterfalls and north Swedish studies are dramatic. But it was not until Richard Bergh (1858-1919), Carl Fredrik Hill (1849-1911) and, above all, Ernst Josephson (1851-1906) that Swedish art, which had largely degenerated into mere *genre* painting, recovered its native vigour. It did so by cross-fertilisation with the Paris school. Both Hill and Josephson died insane, but they are great figures in Swedish art.

A peculiarly pleasing painter and a very Swedish one is the *jugend* painter Carl Larsson (1853-1919). His sensitive cartoons of his own home and family have a charming lightness and grace and innocence about them. Certainly they have survived better than the once famous peasant studies and nudes of Anders

Zorn (1860-1920), who made his fortune in London and the
United States, and whose highly characteristic home, at Mora,
illustrates a whole period of late Swedish romanticism. A good
friend of Zorn—indeed of all the painters of his generation—
was the painter Prince Eugène (1865-1947), brother of the late
King Gustav V. His collections are to be seen at Waldemarsudde
on the outskirts of Stockholm.

Another Swedish artist who made a great name for himself
in the United States was Carl Milles (1875-1955). His flamboy-
ant style seems *passé* today; but it is undeniably genuine and
original, and Milles' great bronze fountain groups—the most
massive of which is the enormous statue of Poseidon in Gothenburg—have a charm and an expressiveness of their own. Full-
scale replicas of the most famous of Milles' work are to be seen
most effectively set out on the garden terraces of Millesgården,
the sculptor's home, just outside the capital, which he left to
the nation.

Among more modern sculptors, Bror Hjorth (1894-1968) is
perhaps the most distinguished. Many of his works are to be
seen in the Gothenburg Museum of Art, which also has a good
collection of post-impressionists.

The present quarrel among Swedish artists—and what would
art be without its quarrels?—is between the dominant abstract
art and the new protagonists of political painting. Discussion
rages as to the merits and demerits of an art which puts left-
wing political affiliation before taste or any other purely artistic
canon. The local authorities, particularly, are finding themselves
in a difficult position, as they do in so many countries. As soon
as their art committee or the superintendent of their art gallery
rejects some artist's work on grounds of its artistic incompetence,
the cry goes up that the said committee or superintendent are
"reactionary" or "fascist."

DESIGN

If Swedes can be said to take the arts more seriously than

most people, and certainly more seriously than people do in Britain or America, they have a positive passion for design. The country produces a startling impression of good, if somewhat formalised taste. Basic to the Swedish style are economy and functionalism. These traits are found in her architecture, in her stainless-steel cutlery, in "Swedish Modern" furniture, in glass, indeed in all the goods of everyday life. Ever since the twenties the conscious goal has been not so much to produce exclusive masterpieces as to create an aesthetically satisfying milieu, integrating beauty with daily living. Items of Swedish glass and furniture, sold as exclusive pieces to the rich in Britain and America, are, in Sweden, within everyone's reach.

Much of the credit for this achievement must go to the Co-operative Movement, with its large network of retail stores. Also to such large department stores as the famous NK (*Nordiska Kompaniet*) in Stockholm, which firmly supported many a creative artist, craftsman and designer, long before there was any fashionable market for such products.

HOMECRAFTS

Sweden has to thank her late industrialisation for many blessings, and one of the more notable is that she never lost her native tradition of crafts and craftsmanship. In the nick of time, before the rising tidewaters of industrialism, and the cheaper machine-made products then being imported from Germany, could sweep them away, and notably thanks to the enthusiasm of such men as Anders Zorn and the Prince Eugène, the traditions were rescued. While the products of the Småland glassworks or a Stockholm jeweller or silversmith are known for distinction's sake as *konstslöjd* (art-craft), the products of thousands of home looms, home workshops and home forges are sold through the nation-wide *Hemslöjdsförbundet* (Swedish Home Crafts League) under the name of *hemslöjd*—home crafts. A *hemslöjd* shop is found in every town and village.

K

These old peasant artifacts, sometimes modernised, sometimes not, fit well into the modern Swedish home, and illustrate the direct continuity which exists between the old tradition and "Swedish Modern." Wrought-iron candlesticks for Christmas candles, cushion covers embroidered in natural-dyed wools, simple and elegant wooden objects like a St Thomas Cross, shaved with a very sharp knife from one clean piece of fine-grained pine wood (but one slip is fatal!)—these and many other bright and pleasant things come from the *hemslöjd* shop. Each region has its traditional wares: pewter from Blekinge, wrought iron from Värmland, reindeer-horn objects from Lapland, etc. The colours are bright, childlike, naïve, but the design is usually clean and well-wrought.

Anyone suffering incapacitation, from an accident or illness for instance, and being obliged to give up his or her normal occupation, is likely to receive a visit from the *Hemslöjdsförbundet* or its local association, which will be only too pleased to train him or her to become a craftsman or craftswoman, spare-time or full-time. In the north, too, where the winter days are short and the snow deep, and farming does not provide livelihood all the year round, many people like to earn extra income in this way. All the work is done on the ancient "putting-out" system, such as existed in pre-industrial Britain. Materials and designs are provided at fixed rates by the association, and the craftsman sells his products also at fixed rates, to the association, which markets them locally, nationally, and even internationally.

THE THEATRE

Of all the arts, theatre and opera are the most heavily subsidised. The most important stage is the Royal Dramatic Theatre (*Dramaten*) in Stockholm. In 1967-68 it received a state grant of Sw. cr. 9.65 million (£770,000, $1.86 million), amounting to 70 per cent of its costs. Total State grants to theatres throughout the country in the previous year amounted to Sw. cr. 55 million (£4.4 million, $11 million). In addition to their share of State support, the seven provincial theatres, of which the most important are in Gothenburg and Malmö—the latter with the largest stage in Europe—also receive heavy municipal subsidies. To serve outlying districts there is the National Touring Theatre (*Riksteatern*), which in 1968 enjoyed a State grant of Sw. cr. 13.6 million (£1.1 million, $2.6 million), as well as contributions from local authorities.

The repertoire is extremely cosmopolitan. It is no exaggeration to say that people living in Stockholm or Gothenburg have a better chance of seeing plays from all countries and translated from many languages than many a theatregoer in London or New York. Many of the plays of Eugène O'Neill, particularly, have had their world premières at *Dramaten*—O'Neill regarding himself as particularly indebted to Strindberg.

About half Sweden's corps of 1,100 actors and actresses are regularly salaried on twelve-month contracts. Recruitment comes from three State-subsidised schools, which together turn out some sixty actors annually; though at present the Swedish actors' financial position compares favourably with that of their foreign colleagues, this total is proving too many.

FILMS

The film industry benefits greatly from its close association with the theatre. Thus Ingmar Bergman, whose name as a director has overshadowed the Swedish film ever since the war, built up during his period as head of the Malmö Theatre a troupe of actors and actresses whom he also used in his most famous films.

Films are usually shot in the summer, while all the theatres are closed. In the days of the great "silents" of the twenties the Swedes were the first film-makers to shoot out of doors, and they have always been notable for fine outdoor camerawork.

It may be asked whether Swedish films, which are sometimes so slanted toward the dark and morbid aspects of life, reflect the realities of Swedish living. Certainly there seems on the face of it something paradoxical about such pessimistic visions coming out of a country whose official social philosophy is so optimistic. But, again, the sudden change in Swedish circumstances has put great stress on the Swedish psyche. Many of the dark threads in Ingmar Bergman's films can be seen as conflicts arising from that psyche being placed in entirely new circumstances, facing demands which its traditional culture was not designed to meet. Certainly the films reflect rather the depths than the surfaces of Swedish life, which are not at all as dramatic as one might infer from the films.

Recently there has been a strong movement away from what one critic calls "Bergman's myth-ridden world." The latest school of film directors is concerned above all with social questions, while Bergman has always been mostly occupied with his own subjective visions; he links up strongly with the Strindbergian tradition. On the other hand, these newer films do not make the same impact on foreign audiences; however deeply Swedish many of the Bergman films may be, they strike a nerve central to modern sensibility everywhere.

The industry has had to struggle with great economic difficulties, and in the early sixties, in spite of its international fame, it nearly had to close down. But in 1963 the cinema entertainment tax was abolished, on condition that for a twenty-year period the industry accepted a self-imposed charge of 10 per cent on all box-office receipts. This is paid to the Swedish Film Institute, which is also State-subsidised, and which uses 35 per cent of its income to support films of high artistic integrity, whose goals are not wholly commercial. A further 30 per cent is spent on artistic training and research, and 5 per cent on the industry's public relations.

MUSIC

Sweden has produced one great symphonic composer, Franz Berwald (1796-1868). But the "father of Swedish music" was the baroque composer Johan Helmich Roman (1694-1758).

Having studied Handel's music in London Roman (pronounced "Rooman") became a composer in the Handelian style, albeit with accents and a personality of his own. Roman's *Drottning-holmsmusique*, in the style of Handel's *Water Music*, is vigorous and charming.

Unlike Roman, Berwald was little appreciated in his own country during his lifetime, and, though he tried to carve a career for himself in Germany, for the most part he had to support himself by running a Swedish gymnastics institute in Berlin or a glassworks in Sweden. The *Sinfonie Sérieuse* and *Sinfonie Singulière*, his two major works, have only recently taken their place in the international repertoire.

Contributing few composers, Sweden has given birth to many more great singers, from the "Swedish Nightingale," Jenny Lind, onwards.

In our own day the most notable are Jussi Björling, the dramatic soprano Birgit Nilsson, the lyrical tenor Nicolai Gedda and the sopranos Kerstin Meyer and Elizabeth Söderström. The Stockholm Opera is noted for the originality and freshness of many of its productions, and another operatic stage, unique in Europe or indeed anywhere, is the eighteenth-century court theatre at Drottningholm, just outside the capital. This is the only perfectly preserved eighteenth-century theatre in the world, and in summer it specialises in performances of opera and ballet from its own day, using the original scenery and stage machinery, still in perfect condition after 200 years.

Of modern composers, the best known are Sven-Erik Bäck, Karl-Birger Blomdahl and Ingvar Lidholm. Blomdahl's "space opera" *Aniara* (1958), to a libretto from a poem by Harry Martinson, is perhaps the most striking literary-musical product to come out of Sweden in the post-war era.

No Swedish symphony orchestra is probably in the top rank internationally, but the four major orchestras, the Stockholm Philharmonic, the Gothenburg Symphony Orchestra, the Opera Orchestra, and the Radio Orchestra, are all of very good standard, the radio orchestra perhaps particularly so. Plans are afoot to provide orchestras in more provincial cities.

The Swedes do not have the British or American tradition of amateur church choirs, theirs being professional and salaried. The radio choir, under Erik Ericsson, has won international acclaim.

Swedish folk music is of two, or even three, distinct sorts. In Darlarna, where the old peasant culture lived on to a late date, and may even be said still to be alive, there is a huge repertoire of country fiddlers' music. Teams of these country fiddlers, dressed in tasselled knee-breeches and frock coats, will play their highly embroidered and ornamented melodies for hours.

Once the ear has grown used to them their polskas and wedding marches are reminiscent of Scottish reels. The *spelmanslåtar*—fiddlers' tunes—are indeed found all over the country and are of earlier date than the romantic songs usually associated with Scandinavian folk music, which mostly date from the nineteenth century. The third category of specifically Swedish popular music is what Swedes call *gammaldans*—"old dance music." The instruments here are the accordion and clarinet, and the repertoire, which is vast, consists of waltzes, schottisches, polkas etc. Monotonous and even somewhat simple-minded, this sort of music nevertheless has a certain charm when heard in its natural habitat—out by some calm lake on a light midsummer night, where couples are dancing to its strains on a wooden jetty. It is this atmosphere and this music which Hugo Alfven (1872-1960) tried to evoke in his internationally popular *Swedish Rhapsody*, the original title of which is *Midsommarvaka* —*A Midsummer Night's Vigil*.

9

Hints For Visitors

FIRST, a visit to Sweden is always likely to be more rewarding in the summertime (May-August). If on business, on the other hand, it is useless to go there at the height of the summer (July), because then everyone is away on holiday. A good time to combine both sorts of visit is the end of August, or in May-June. The working year begins in September, and it is then that the Swedes are most prepared to look forward to new projects and fresh ideas. The dark season (November to February) is both cold and oppressive. At the end of the winter, too (March to April), a general lassitude makes itself felt. The spring arrives in May, with new life.

A visitor should try to range beyond Stockholm, which certainly contains enough sights to occupy at least three days profitably, but is also more expensive than the rest of the country. Regions well worth exploring are Dalarna (Dalecarlia), which lies only four to five hours north from Stockholm by road or rail; the medieval city of Visby, on Gotland; the chateau country of Skåne, in the far south; and, for wonderfully good bathing and long hours of summer sunshine, the west coast. This coast has two parts: south of Gothenburg for shallow sandy beaches, and north of it for the picturesque and altogether characteristic Bohuslän archipelago. Both these areas are well-stocked with Swedish holidaymakers in July, but swiftly become depopulated in mid-August.

To do as the Swedes do, and rent a summer chalet is much to be recommended. Great numbers of these chalets, both individual and built in clusters (*semesterbyar*), are available at attractive spots along the coast, by lakes or in the countryside, or in the mountains of the north. In July they are not quite so easily rented, being mostly occupied by Swedes. Purpose-built, these summer houses contain bunks, a kitchenette with electric cooker and refrigerator, and all things needful for a holiday except linen, which the tourist brings for himself. The rent is usually subsidised by the State in one way or another, and is therefore surprisingly low for the standard of the dwelling. In the north the chalets are also used for winter sports.

The Swedes are hardly a chummy people, at least not on the surface. But unaffected friendliness will thaw them out. Excessive heartiness, however, is only apt to make a Swede feel still more shy and retiring.

Most things are organised in Sweden, and there is an efficient organisation for helping foreign visitors to make personal contact with like-minded Swedes. It is called "Sweden at Home," and has on its lists some 800 families who speak foreign languages, mostly English, and who are happy to welcome a visitor to their homes for coffee—sometimes for a meal. On the other hand, accommodation cannot always be arranged in this way; as has been explained, Swedish flats are usually fairly small, and do not have guest rooms. Application to any Swedish tourist office abroad* will open up this road into Swedish realities. "Sweden at Home" offices exist in Stockholm and a dozen other cities.

When invited to a Swedish home it is customary to take a bunch of flowers or a box of chocolates for one's hostess. If invited to dinner, then a certain nodding acquaintance with the formalities of such an occasion is desirable. Each gentleman takes a lady by the arm to lead her to table (your hostess will tell you where to sit). He does not drink without first saying "skål," either to her or to some other guest. (Not, however, to his hostess, whose privilege it is to decide with whom she wishes to drink). If you are the guest of honour and sitting on your

* In London: The Swedish National Travel Association, 52/53 Conduit Street, W1. In New York: Scandinavian Travel Commission, Fifth Avenue.

hostess's immediate left, then you will be expected towards the end of the meal, to make a small speech of gratitude for the dinner, on your own and your fellow-guests' behalf. Afterwards, shake hands with your hostess and say *"tack för maten"* —thanks for the dinner.

If you meet her in the street several days or even weeks afterwards, say *"tack för sist"*—thanks for last time.

Punctuality is absolute in Sweden, both socially and in business. If invited for dinner at six—Swedes dine early—then that is the exact moment to ring the front-door bell.

When eating out, good, quick meals can be obtained from the spacious and elegant self-service cafeterias, found everywhere, among other places in department stores (EPA, Ringbaren, etc.) They serve wine and beer, but not spirits. Grill-bars also serve lavish portions, and, as they are run by Italians and Spaniards, service is brisk.

Not so in a real Swedish restaurant, where it can take an astonishingly long time to get served, and even longer to get the bill afterwards. When it comes, it is liable to be pretty hefty—everything in Sweden that involves labour is expensive. A Swedish waitress takes home at least £100 ($250) a month, and she expects a 12 per cent tip, which she simply adds to the bill. Taxi drivers expect 10 per cent or more, but give cheerful service in exchange. When sightseeing in Stockholm, your hotel porter will, if you ask him, order a taxi-guide— a taxi whose chauffeur has been trained as a guide and speaks one of any number of languages. This will cost no more than an ordinary taxi.

One of the classic tourist ways of Sweden is the 100-year-old Göta Canal, which joins up the great lakes of central Sweden. The three-day trip goes from Gothenburg to Stockholm or viceversa, and only about a quarter of it is actually through the old canal. The ships are small and old, but very clean, the food good, and the trip, which seems endless, altogether memorable.

The midnight sun, which Sweden and Norway, Finland and Russia, all share, can be seen north of the Arctic Circle—reached by electric train—between mid-May and mid-July. The best time to visit Lapland is in the latter part of June, before the mosquitoes come, or in August, after the first frosts have killed them off and turned the great expanses of Arctic vegetation a brilliant scarlet.

Index

Index

Hospitals, 81, 82, 83, 84
Housing, 63-7, 71, 80
Huskvarna Co, 105

Ice hockey, 142
Immigration, 17
Incomes, 73
Industrialisation, 19
Industry,
  localisation of, 90-1
  state-owned, 89
Iron mining, 26, 89, 91, 96, 103-4

Jämtland, 14
Jarring, Gunnar, 54
Jews, 17
Johan III, 27
Johansson, C. E., 106
Josephson, Ernst, 151
Judiciary, 45
Juvenile courts, 50

Kalmar, 130
Kalmar Union, 26
Karl XIV Johan, 29
Karlfeldt, E. A., 48
Kiruna, 103
Kitchens, 66
Kommuner, 41
Kreuger, Ivar, 31

Labour Court, 45, 95
Labour-management committees, 96
Labour relations, 92, 93, 94, 95
Lagerlöf, Selma, 148
Lakes, 11
Landshövding, 42
Lapland, 11, 20, 70, 90, 103, 104, 125, 162
Lapps, 17-18
Larson, Carl, 151
Larson, Marcus, 151

Law, 46, 47
Legislation, process of, 37-9
Liberal Party, 36
Lidholm, Ingvar, 157
Lidman, Sarah, 139
Lind, Jenny, 157
Lindgren, Eric, 149
Linnaeus, Carl, 14, 28
Literature, 147-9
Local government, 41-4, 47
Luleå, 70, 104
Lund, 15, 116, 118, 135

Mälaren, Lake, 15, 26
Malmö, 13, 41, 69, 107, 126, 130, 155
Martin, Elias, 29, 151
Martinson, Harry, 157
Match industry, 100, 103
Medelpad, 14
Medicine, 81-4
Merchant marine, 130
Meyer, Kerstin, 157
Midnight sun, 12, 161
Midsummer, 76, 141
Milles, Carl, 152
Mo & Domsjö AB, 92, 109
Moberg, Vilhelm, 149
Motoring, 125-7
Music, 156-8
Myrdal, Jan, 139

Närke, 14
Navy, 57, 58
Newspapers, 71, 131, 143-6
Nilsson, Birgit, 157
NK (Nordiska Kompaniet), 153
Nobel, Alfred, 109, 147
Nobel Prizes, 146-7, 148
Norrland, 14, 20, 91, 99, 111, 137
Norrbotten, 14, 20, 55
Notke, Bernt, 150-1

DATE DUE

FE 4 '81			
MR 23 '82			
JA 30 '83			
JAN 30 '87			
FEB 13 '87			
FEB 29 '87			
MAR 25 '87			
FEB 14 '89			
FEB 28 '89			
GAYLORD			PRINTED IN U.S.A.